GW00402086

Palliative D
Care in Prac

Palliative Day Care in Practice

Julie Hearn
Senior Executive
National Cancer Research Institute
Clinical Studies Groups, London, U.K.

and

Kathryn Myers
Macmillan Consultant in Palliative Medicine,
The Peace Hospice, Watford, U.K.

OXFORD
UNIVERSITY PRESS

OXFORD
UNIVERSITY PRESS

Great Clarendon Street, Oxford OX2 6DP

Oxford University Press is a department of the University of Oxford.
It furthers the University's objective of excellence in research, scholarship,
and education by publishing worldwide in

Oxford New York

Auckland Bangkok Buenos Aires Cape Town Chennai
Dar es Salaam Delhi Hong Kong Istanbul Karachi Kolkata
Kuala Lumpur Madrid Melbourne Mexico City Mumbai Nairobi
São Paulo Shanghai Taipei Tokyo Toronto

Oxford is a registered trade mark of Oxford University Press
in the UK and in certain other countries

Published in the United States
by Oxford University Press Inc., New York

© Oxford University Press 2001

The moral rights of the author have been asserted
Database right Oxford University Press (maker)

First published 2001
Reprinted 2002 (with corrections)

British Library Cataloguing in Publication Data
Data available

Library of Congress Cataloging in Publication Data
Data available

ISBN 0 19 263183 7 (Pbk)

Typeset in Minion by Florence Production Ltd
Printed in Great Britain
on acid-free paper by Biddles Ltd, Guildford & King's Lynn

Foreword

In the United Kingdom it often seems that the provision of hospice and palliative day care holds a special place within the overall palliative care philosophy. First established in Sheffield in 1975, the idea of hospice day care was seen at that time as a day out for the patient and a day off for the carer. Interestingly, just over a generation later, it was also in Sheffield that we saw the first closure of a palliative day care service. Over the years, I have been in discussions where protagonists have argued fiercely for the importance of palliative day care. I have also witnessed great variations in what day care is understood to be by those who provide it. On one occasion I enquired into the costs of day care provision in my own area and was rather surprised by the huge variations between services in the same locality. When visiting day units I have observed facilities of various kinds: in converted cottages and purpose-built centres; where the 'social model' has been espoused; where doctors may or may not be involved actively; where opportunities for pain and symptom management were quickly seized upon by the staff; or where the 'guests' saw themselves as simply attending an enjoyable lunch club.

Hospice and palliative day care provision has expanded rapidly in the UK, but it is not an example that has been much followed by others in Europe. Certainly the roots of day care seem caught up in notions of sociability and association which are so important within the British culture of charitable endeavour. It may therefore hold less appeal where norms of family care are stronger or, conversely, where state-provided health care is primarily associated with the work of the poly-clinic or the acute hospital. It remains to be seen whether it will be given much priority in the expanding programmes of palliative care now being developed in many countries of the world.

For all these reasons, *Palliative Day Care in Practice* is a very timely book. It lifts the lid on a cherished value of palliative care in the UK and asks some important questions. Readers will gain valuable insight into the diversity of elements that can make up palliative day care, not least the heady mixture of creative, practical and therapeutic processes which it may involve. They will also be asked to consider how we assess the 'need' for such care at a population level. They will obtain an understanding of how these services are designed and established, as well as the day to day problems faced in their delivery. Above all they will be challenged by the absence of evaluation evidence concerning what day care is and what it achieves. In this respect of course, palliative day care may be seen as no more than an extreme case within the overall context of a specialty which is lacking an evidence base. But when, as the authors here claim, we are dealing with the most rapidly expanding area of palliative care provision (at least in the UK), then clearly it is a cause for concern. *Palliative Day Care in Practice* therefore joins a small collection of palliative care books that adopt a critical and challenging orientation to their subject matter. As a result it may make uncomfortable reading. Let us hope it will also stimulate both the providers of services and those concerned with evaluation to become both clearer and more informed about this aspect of palliative care provision.

Professor David Clark
University of Sheffield

Preface

Palliative day care is one of the most rapidly expanding components of palliative care in the UK, and is increasingly a focus of new service development in other parts of the world. Many benefits, in terms of improving quality of life, providing a holistic approach to the care of both the patient and the family, and facilitating increased time at home, are claimed by day care. There has, however, been little research to substantiate these claims and few studies and evaluations of palliative day care have been published compared with other palliative care services such as home or inpatient care.

The editors recognized the need for a textbook that took an analytical approach to the provision of palliative day care whilst designing and establishing a multi-centre evaluation of palliative day care in the UK. This book attempts to take such an approach, and to provide a comprehensive overview of the current literature on the philosophies, patterns and policies of palliative day care. Each chapter is grounded as far as possible in evidence drawn from palliative care research in general and from palliative day care specifically, where this is available. The authors are all able to draw on extensive experience of the provision of palliative day care services and have all participated in research in the day care setting.

The book is divided into four parts. The first part aims to define palliative day care by describing its history and the current profile of service provision, and to set this in the context of needs assessment and the importance of equitable service provision for people from a diversity of ethnic groups. The second part considers the provision of care, describing the parameters to be considered when establishing a service, and illustrating the diversity of approaches to care by the description of two very different services. Part three aims to introduce the reader to the systematic appraisal of palliative day care by providing information on audit in palliative care and the potential of health economic evaluation. The final part presents challenges for palliative day care in the future.

Palliative day care is a complex service. It attempts to address patients' physical, psychological, social and spiritual needs within an environment that acknowledges individuality and the need for flexibility. No two services are the same, and it is unlikely that any two patients will recieve exactly the same services. This in itself presents considerable challenges for the researcher. The population, however, is ageing and hence an increasing number of older people will be living with cancer and other life-threatening diseases in the future. Demands for palliative care, including (perhaps especially) palliative day care are likely to increase. The emphasis of this book is the need continuously to question and improve care to meet the needs of both patients and purchasers of palliative care services in the future. We hope that by providing an extensive literature review, addressing topics relevant to the provision of care, and highlighting the difficulties in conducting research, the reader will be able to base future practice and research on the pertinent evidence available. As a result, we hope that future services will be able to meet the needs of the greatest numbers of people in the most effective ways.

Ms Julie Hearn
Dr Kathy Myers

Acknowledgements

With thanks to our families for their support and encouragement, and to all those involved in the Thames Regional Palliative Day Care study.

Ms Julie Hearn
Dr Kathy Myers

Contents

Foreword by David Clark *v*

Preface *vii*

Contributor List *x*

Part A. **Defining day care**

1 An introduction to palliative day care: past and present *1*
Kathryn Myers and Julie Hearn

2 Needs assessment in day care *12*
Irene J. Higginson and Danielle M. Goodwin

3 Working across cultures of difference: ethnicity and the challenge for palliative day care *23*
Yasmin Gunaratnam

Part B. **Providing day care**

4 Establishing day care *43*
Karon O'Keefe

5 Psychosocial day care *59*
Cynthia Kennett

6 The role of the doctor in day care *79*
Adrian J. Tookman and Karen S. Scharpen-von Heussen

Part C. **Evaluating day care**

7 Audit in palliative day care: what, why, when, how, where and who *94*
Julie Hearn

8 The role of health economics *116*
Hannah-Rose Douglas and Charles Normand

Part D. **Challenges for day care**

9 Future perspectives for day care *136*
Kathryn Myers

Index *153*

Contributor List

Ms Hannah-Rose Douglas
London School of Hygiene an
  Tropical Medicine
Health Services Research Unit
Keppel Street
London WC2A

Ms Danielle Goodwin
Guy's, King's and St. Thomas'
  School of Medicine and St.
  Christopher's Hospice
  Department of Palliative Care
  and Policy
Weston Education Centre
Cutcombe Road
Denmark Hill
London SE5 9RJ

Dr Yasmin Gunaratnam
School of Health and Social Welfare
The Open University
Walton Hall
Milton Keynes
MK7 6AA

Professor Irene Higginson
Guy's, King's and St. Thomas'
  School of Medicine and St.
  Christopher's Hospice
  Department of Palliative Care
  and Policy
Weston Education Centre
Cutcombe Road
Denmark Hill
London SE5 9RJ

Ms Cynthia Kennett
St. Christopher's Hospice
51–59 Lawrie Park Road
Sydenham
London SE26 6DZ

Professor Charles Normand
London School of Hygiene and
  Tropical Medicine
Health Services Research Unit
Keppel Street
London WC2A

Ms Karon O'Keefe
Sacred Heart Palliative Care Service
170 Darlinghurst Road
NSW 2010
Australia

Dr Karen Scharpen von Heussen
Edenhall Marie Curie Centre
11 Lyndhurst Gardens
Hamstead
London NW3 5NS

Dr Adrian Tookman
Royal Free Hospital NHS Trust
Pond Street
London NW3 2QG
  and
Edenhall Marie Curie Centre
11 Lyndhurst Gardens
Hamstead
London NW3 5NS

PART A.   DEFINING DAY CARE

1

An introduction to palliative day care: past and present

Kathryn Myers and Julie Hearn

Introduction

From small beginnings in the 1960s the hospice movement in the United Kingdom has burgeoned. At the beginning of the twenty-first century palliative care services inspired by the hospice ethos are available nationally and their numbers are increasing internationally. Difficult questions, however, are being asked and palliative care is under fire. Criticisms that services provide 'luxury dying' for a few have been levelled (Douglas1992) and the need for 'specialist' palliative care at all has been questioned (Fordham *et al.* 1998). In a climate of evidence-based medicine and limited financial resources, palliative care services are under greater pressure than ever before to demonstrate both their effectiveness and cost-effectiveness.

This book attempts to address some of these issues with respect to the fastest growing but least researched component of palliative care services: palliative day care. It is not a manual on how to set up and run a palliative day care service. Rather, it represents an attempt to 'chart the territory' of palliative day care in the United Kingdom. For readers new to the field it aims to survey the broad concepts and components of palliative day care and the philosophies and practical issues that relate to them. For those more experienced in the field, it seeks to highlight some of the questions, challenges and dilemmas that palliative day care services face and will need to address in the years ahead.

Numerous definitions of services abound in the field of palliative care. We cite in box 1 the definitions published by the World Health Organisation (WHO) and National Council for Hospice and Specialist Palliative Care Services (NCHSPCS) as these are in most frequent use. Defining a difference, however, between specialist palliative care services and those provided by hospices, is largely a theoretical exercise. In practice, many specialist services in settings outside hospices share the philosophy of

Box 1 Definitions

Palliative care

- The active total care of patients and their families by a multiprofessional team when the patient's disease is no longer responsive to curative treatment (World Health Organisation 1990).
- Palliative care services is a broad term which covers provision in both community and inpatient settings. Services may be NHS or voluntary, multi-professional or uniprofessional; and may be provided by individuals or teams. Some may meet the definition of specialist palliative care services, others may not; they are all staffed by professionals who have extensive experience and/or additional training in aspects of palliative care, some up to specialist level (Wiles 1995).
- Specialist palliative care services are those services with palliative care as their core speciality (Wiles 1995).
- Hospice and hospice care refer to a philosophy of care rather than a specific building or service and may encompass a programme of care and array of skills deliverable in a wide range of settings. However, the range and quality of the services are not defined by the use of the term (Wiles 1995).

Specialist palliative day care

- The function of specialist palliative day care is to enhance the quality of life of patients through rehabilitation, physiotherapy and occupational therapy, the management and monitoring of symptoms and the provision of psychosocial support (Tebbit 1990).

Hospice palliative day care

- The function of hospice palliative day care is to enhance the quality of life of patients through activities which include the following:
  1) social interactions, mutual support and friendship
  2) creative and therapeutic activities
  3) clinical surveillance and physical care, such as bathing
  4) respite for home carers (Tebbit 1999).

hospice, and many hospices aim to provide high quality specialist palliative care services.

Palliative day care—diversity, complexity and flexibility

The provision of rehabilitation and medical treatment through day care
services is not unique to palliative care. Day care is well established in the
care of the elderly and psychiatric services, in haematology and oncology,
and in some surgical specialties. These tend however, to focus on specific
therapeutic interventions and none of these would claim to be as broad
in their scope and philosophy as palliative day care.

The first purpose built palliative day care centre opened at St Luke's
hospice in Sheffield in 1975 to support patients with pre-terminal cancer
and chronic disease (Wilkes 1978). Although it was the first centre of its
kind, St Luke's included all the components of specialist palliative day care
described in more recent definitions (Box 1). It also shared much with
modern day care centres in its philosophy. In common with palliative care
services in other settings, palliative day care has from its inception recognised that patients' physical, emotional, social and spiritual needs cannot
usually be compartmentalised but are often inextricably intertwined. In
attempting to address these needs, palliative day care centres put a high
priority on:

- acknowledging patients' uniqueness and individuality;
- promoting independence and enhancing quality of life through control
  of symptoms and rehabilitation;
- psychological support aimed at improving strategies for dealing with
  stress, anxiety and depression and increasing self esteem and confidence;
- engendering hope and meaning;
- relief of social isolation and provision of respite for carers;
- co-ordination of the health and social care networks involved in patients'
  care.

Clearly, these aims are ambitious and wide-ranging and it is not therefore suprising that most palliative day care services are complex in their
structure and functioning. Multi-disciplinary team working is essential to
this approach and services must be characterised by flexibility if patients'
individual needs are to be met (Thompson 1990, Biswas and Johnson
1992). Palliative day care services have evolved with different emphases
in part because of differing access to resources and different populations
in different localities. This has resulted in a wide diversity of services and

models of care (Faulkner 1993). In 1994 it was suggested that day care services might form a spectrum, some being more medical in emphasis, others being more social (Eve and Smith 1994). Recent research suggests that palliative day care services share common core components upon which others are then built in diverse ways (Douglas 2000). Chapters 5 and 6 in this book serve to illustrate this diversity in practice. Chapter 5 (Psychosocial Day Care, Kennett) gives an account of the model of day care practised at St Christopher's Hospice in South London, which is geared to the psychosocial wellbeing of patients. Chapter 6 (The Role of the Doctor in Day Care, Scharpen-von Heussen and Tookman) illustrates the practice of the Edenhall Marie Curie Day Therapy Unit where medical care has a significant role.

The implications of the diversity of palliative care provision in terms of which components of care are the most effective, for which groups of patients and under what circumstances, have yet to be fully explored.

From philosophy to practice

Palliative day care provision in the United Kingdom

The last decade has witnessed a major expansion in the provision of palliative day care services in the UK. In 1991 there were 151 palliative day care services attended by approximately 4500 different patients each week (Eve and Smith 1994). By January 2000 there were 243 palliative day care services (more than the number of inpatient palliative care services) attended by an estimated 9000 patients per week (Hospice facts and figures 2000) (Fig. 1.1). The reasons for such an increase in provision are not

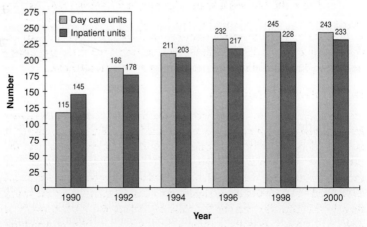

Fig. 1.1 Growth in palliative care services in the UK, 1990–2000.

entirely clear. During the last ten years there has undoubtedly been a greater recognition at government level of the need for palliative care services. At the same time, successive reports on palliative care provision have emphasised the need to expand community palliative care services and to integrate them with inpatient palliative care units and general practice in order to provide a 'seamless service' for patients (SNAC/SNMAC 1992; Department of Health 1995).

In the absence of a national strategy for development of palliative care services, much of the expansion in palliative day care may have happened anyway, on the grounds that palliative day care is self-evidently 'a good thing'. Numerous local factors such as funding and the involvement, enthusiasm and influence of different types of health care professionals may have been influential. New developments in palliative care services in the United Kingdom have frequently relied heavily on such local initiatives, often through the local voluntary sector (Clark *et al.* 1997). Whilst this has enabled provision of services that might not otherwise be affordable, such initiatives have not always been based on rigorous needs assessments (Faulkner 1993).

An equal concern in the development of palliative day care is that such a huge expansion in services has happened largely in the absence of evidence to support its effectiveness. The Scottish Partnership Agency for example, (Scottish Partnership Agency 1995) recommended that there should be one day care place per 10 000 of the population with an optimum number of 20 places per centre, although the evidence for this recommendation is not apparent. Although anecdotal reports of the benefits of palliative day care are numerous, literature relating to its evaluation and cost-effectiveness is sparse (Spencer and Daniels 1998). As purchasers of health care services in the UK seek to be increasingly efficient in their deployment of scarce resources, palliative day care services are coming under increasing pressure to demonstrate both their responsiveness to local needs and their effectiveness in meeting those needs.

International provision

Provision of palliative care services across the world varies enormously from country to country. Where services are being developed, however, it is usually inpatient and home care services that take priority, as was the case in the UK twenty years ago. Palliative day care services have been reported in the USA, Australia, Japan as well as in several European countries (Clark *et al.* 2000) but are significantly less common across the world than in the UK. The reasons for this may reflect the relative youth of palliative care as a specialty in some countries or very different structures of providing and funding palliative care services.

It would be unwise to assume, however, that palliative day care as it exists in the UK can be transferred easily into other cultural settings, or indeed that any such transfer is desirable. It may be that as palliative care services develop in other countries and cultures, new innovations in models of service delivery will emerge that will challenge, enrich and inspire those that are more established.

Characteristics of palliative day care services

Two recent surveys have attempted to 'map' palliative day care services in the UK by describing their characteristics in detail. The first (Copp *et al.* 1998), a telephone survey of 131 palliative day care centres from 17 regions of the UK, enquired about types of service provision, management and organisational issues and the nature of problems of patients attending. The second, the Thames regions palliative day care study, surveyed 43 palliative day care services from the North and South Thames regions using a written questionnaire. This aimed to map the diversity of services available and to explore evidence that might support the hypothesis that 'medical' and 'social' models of palliative day care exist (Higginson *et al.* 2000). These surveys demonstrated that by far the largest proportion of patients attending palliative day care centres have a diagnosis of cancer (90% in Higginson *et al.*) and are in the age range 61–80 years (Copp *et al.*). Reasons for referral to day care and the types of support offered were various, with social interaction, psychological support, respite for carers and monitoring and symptom control featuring commonly.

Both surveys demonstrated diversity amongst centres with respect to characteristics such as size (16–150 places per centre per week), the total number of patients cared for (26–1526 patients per year) and opening hours (9–49 hours per week, mainly on weekdays). Very few centres opened at weekends or 'out of hours'. Some operated drop-in services. Some set aside particular days for younger patients. Sources of funding varied, with some being independently funded, others entirely NHS funded and others being funded by both. Most centres were managed by nurses and most, but by no means all, had access to doctors. A wide variety of other services were available, for example, physiotherapists, occupational therapists, chaplains, aromatherapists, dieticians, music and art therapists, social workers and volunteers, though not all centres had access to all of these and not all had access at all times. It is possible to envisage how different patients might receive different types of service depending upon which palliative day centre they attend, or even, within a single centre, on which day of the week they attend.

Proponents of palliative day care have pointed out however, that palliative day care is more than a collection of individual services. Rather, many palliative day care centres aim to provide an environment wherein patients can interact with staff and with other patients, and this interaction may in itself be therapeutic (Langley-Evans and Payne 1997).

The Thames regions palliative day care study has subsequently carried out a detailed prospective study of five palliative day care centres using both quantitative and qualitative research methods. Amongst other things, it aimed to provide data about the structure and processes of day care, its effectiveness and cost-effectiveness, and to explore the impact of day care services on patients' quality of life and use of other health care and social services. Several authors contributing to this book have been involved in this research and publication of results began in 2000 (Higginson *et al.* 2000, Douglas *et al.* 2000).

Relationship to other services

The palliative day care centre has been described as the hub of community palliative care, bridging the interface between home care services and specialist inpatient units so that patients can be referred smoothly from one to the other as they require (Fisher and McDaid 1996). In this model, palliative day care is part of a fully integrated, comprehensive palliative care service that incorporates community palliative care and inpatient services and which is easily accessed by medical and nursing professionals from both community and acute sectors. The extent to which this reflects current practice, however, has not been fully assessed. In the survey by Copp *et al.* (1998) 35% of centres had links with both an inpatient hospice unit and a home care team but 11% had links with neither. Higginson *et al.* (2000) found that whilst in three centres all patients were referred to day care by specialist palliative care nurses working in the community, in three others, none were referred by this route. Other referrers included family practitioners, hospice nurses and doctors, hospital staff nurses and district nurses.

Whether a palliative day care centre is part of an integrated palliative care service or not, its relationship with the health care professionals that refer to it may have a major role in determining which patients receive palliative day care and which do not. Misconceptions about the terms 'day care' and 'hospice' may be a barrier to some professionals referring to palliative day care services, as well as preventing some patients from accepting care.

It is interesting that there is great diversity in the titles chosen for palliative day care centres. This in itself might be a reflection of the different emphases and models of care that exist. Some readily use the term 'day hospice'. Others have avoided it, apparently to avoid negative connotations that some patients might attach to the term 'hospice'. Yet others have avoided the term 'day centre', to prevent confusion with day care provided by social services or departments for care of the elderly. Potential referrers may unwittingly 'gate-keep' unless fully informed about the nature of palliative day care services. Services therefore need to publicise and market themselves through education of other health care professionals if they are to gain access to the patients they are designed to help.

Conversely, palliative day care centres need to retain sufficiently broad referral criteria to ensure that patients who might benefit from palliative day care are not excluded. Failure may result in patients being forced to fit into services rather than services being truly shaped by patients' needs. In the survey by Higginson *et al.* (2000) all centres contacted had critieria for admitting patients to day care and these commonly included being terminally ill or having active and progressive disease and having physical, emotional and social needs for support. The most common reasons for patients being refused day care were behavioural problems, having a diagnosis that did not fit with stated criteria or being unable to be transported to the centre. As palliative care services are challenged to broaden their scope to include those dying from diseases other than cancer, palliative day care services might be called upon increasingly to extend and adapt their services to patients who might never previously have been referred to them. The challenge of 'generic' palliative day care will be addressed more fully in chapter 9.

Impact on other services

Although potentially at the hub of a 'seamless' palliative care service no data on the impact of palliative day care on the use of other palliative care services has yet been published. Claims have been made that, through monitoring of patients and pre-empting problems, attendance at a palliative day care centre might reduce the number of admissions to both hospitals and inpatient palliative care units. On the other hand, it is possible to envisage how the converse might occur. Attendance at day care may lead to patients' problems being identified at an earlier stage. Some staff might have a lower threshold for requesting admission for patients they know well through day care and some patients might be happier to be admitted to a hospice that they are familiar with through day care rather than choosing to stay at home. In their chapter on the role of the doctor in palliative day care Tookman and Scharpen-von Heussen describe how the number of planned admissions to inpatient care increased through the monitoring activities of a palliative day therapy unit. The impact of palliative day care attendance on emergency admissions has not been evaluated.

The effect that attendance at a palliative day care centre has on patients' use of other community health services, for example the family doctor and district nurse, and on use of social services is being explored by the Thames regions palliative day care study. For some, palliative day care may be a supplementary form of care. For others it may substitute for other forms of care. In practice, whichever is the case for a particular patient, efficient communication with other professionals is essential to ensure that patients do not fall through gaps in the service 'net' when their circumstances change. This is particularly true for many patients with advanced cancer whose disease and needs can change significantly within a short period of time. It is also true for those whose disease stabilises and who no longer need specialist palliative day care. Some palliative day care services have great difficulties in discharging patients who may no longer need their specialist support. In the study by Higginson *et al.* (2000) the mean time that the longest-attending patient had been coming to day care was 4.5 years (range 1–12 years). The reasons why it may be difficult to discharge patients from day care have not been researched but are doubtless complex. They are often compounded, however, by the lack of suitable alternative forms of day care, particularly social day care, to which patients can be referred.

Evaluation of palliative day care

The need to evaluate palliative day care along with other aspects of palliative care services has been voiced almost since its inception (Wilkes 1980) and on numerous occasions subsequently (for example, Faulkner 1993). It is therefore concerning that a recent book aiming 'to identify the most appropriate and cost-effective model of service delivery and level of provision of palliative care services' by means of a comprehensive literature review, was unable to cite a single report of an evaluative study of palliative day care (Bosanquet and Salisbury 1999).

The reasons why such evaluation, so strongly called for in such a rapidly expanding field, has not been carried out previously are speculative. The benefits of day care attendance for some patients may have been so self-evident in some services that formal evaluation has had low priority. There is certainly no shortage of such anecdotal reports in the literature. It may be that a lack of financial resources, time and expertise in research methodology and the complexity of the task have all contributed. The small size and independent funding of many palliative day care services would make comprehensive evaluation a daunting task. Academic centres able to co-ordinate multicentre projects and provide expertise are a relatively recent development in palliative care.

Clearly, evaluation of palliative day care is not easy, but neither should it be impossible. In her chapter on audit, Hearn describes tested ways in which individual services can use audit to examine their practices. Douglas and Normand highlight the contribution that health economics can make in their chapter on economic evaluation. In the final chapter Myers explores the many challenges faced by researchers in palliative day care and some of the key questions that need to be researched.

Many of those experienced in working in the field of palliative day care are in no doubt about its effectiveness. One of the many challenges ahead is to demonstrate and describe this effectiveness. This will be essential not only if palliative day care services are to be sure that they are serving as many patients as appropriately as possible in future, but also if they are to receive the support and resources they will need to do so.

Summary points

+ Palliative day care is the fastest growing but least researched component of palliative care services.
+ There is a wide diversity of provision between services with some being more medical and some more social in approach.
+ Palliative day care is a complex service with emphasis on addressing patients' physical, psychological, social and spiritual needs within an environment that acknowledges individuality and the need for flexibility.
+ The impact of palliative day care provision on the use of other palliative care, health and social services has not been evaluated.
+ Evaluation of palliative day care is not easy but is essential if services are to be targeted effectively and resourced adequately in future.

References

Biswas, B. and Johnson, P. (1992). Interviews with Bronwen Biswas and Phina Johnson. *Journal of Cancer Care*, 1, 217–21.

Bosanquet, N. and Salisbury, C. (1999). *Providing a palliative care service. Towards an evidence base.* Oxford University Press, Oxford.

Clark, D., Hockley, J. and Ahmedzai, S.(eds) (1997). *New themes in palliative care,* p62. Open University Press, Buckingham UK and Bristol, Philadelphia, USA.

Clark, D., ten Have, H.A.M.J., Janssens, R.J.P.A.(2000) Common threads? Palliative care service developments in seven European countries. *Palliative Medicine* 2000, 14, 479–90.

Copp, G., Richardson, A., McDaid, P. and Marshall-Searson, D.A. (1998). A telephone survey of the provision of palliative day care services. *Palliative Medicine*, 12, 161–70.

Department of Health. (1995). *A policy framework for commissioning cancer services.* A report by the Expert Advisory group on cancer to the Chief Medical Officer of England and Wales. Department of Health and Welsh Office London.

Douglas, C. (1992). For all the saints. *British Medical Journal,* **304**, 579.

Douglas, H-R., Higginson I.J., Myers, K. and Normand, C. (2000). Assessing structure, process and outcome in palliative day care: a pilot study for a multicentre trial. *Health and Social Care in the Community,* **8(5)**, 336–344.

Eve, A. and Smith, A.M. (1994). Palliative care services in Britain and Ireland – update 1991. *Palliative Medicine,* **8**, 19–27.

Eve, A., Smith A.M. and Tebbit P. (1997). Hospice and palliative care in the UK 1994–5, including a summary of trends 1990–5. *Palliative Medicine,* **11**, 31–43

Faulkner, A., Higginson, I., Egerton, H., Power, M., Sykes, N. and Wilkes, E. (1993). *Hospice day care: a qualitative study.* Trent Palliative Care Centre and Help the Hospices, Sheffield.

Fisher, R.A. and McDaid, P. (1996). *Palliative day care.* Arnold, London.

Fordham, S., Dowrick, C. and May, C. (1998). Palliative medicine: is it really specialist territory? *Journal of the Royal Society of Medicine,* **91**, 568–72

Higginson, I.H., Hearn, J., Myers, K., Naysmith, A. (2000). Palliative day care: what do services do? *Palliative Medicine* **14**, 277–286.

Hospice and Palliative Care facts and figures 2000. The Hospice Information Service, St Christopher's Hospice, London.

Langley-Evans, A. and Payne, S. (1997). Light-hearted death talk in a palliative day care context. *Journal of Advanced Nursing,* **26**, 1091–7.

Scottish Partnership Agency. (1995) Scottish partnership agency for palliative and cancer care. Day hospice report of a meeting of the health service group of the Scottish partnership agency for palliative care. Scottish Partnership Agency, Edinburgh.

SMAC/SNMAC (Standing Medical Advisory Committee and Standing Nursing and Midwifery Advisory Committee) (1992). *The principles and provision of palliative care.* HMSO, London.

Spencer, D.J. and Daniels, L.E. (1998). Day hospice care – a review of the literature. *Palliative Medicine,* **12**, 219–29.

Tebbit, P. (1999). Palliative Care 2000. Commissioning through Partnership. National Council for Hospice and Specialist Palliative Care Services, London.

Thompson, B., (1990). Hospice day care. *American Journal of Hospice Care,* **1**, 28–30.

Wiles, J. (1995) *Specialist palliative care: a statement of definitions.* Occasional paper 8. National Council for Hospice and Specialist Palliative Care Services, London.

Wilkes, E., Crowther, A.G.O., Greaves, C.W.K.H. (1978). A different kind of day hospital for patients with preterminal cancer and chronic disease. *British Medical Journal,* **2**, 1053–6.

Wilkes, E. (1980). Department of Health and Social Security. Report of the working group on terminal care. HMSO, London.

World Health Organisation. (1990). Technical Report Series 804. WHO, Geneva.

2

Needs assessment in day care

Irene J. Higginson and
Danielle M. Goodwin

Introduction: what is needs assessment?

An important aspect of the effectiveness of a service is the extent to which
it matches the demands and needs of the population. Barker *et al.* (1998)
suggest that demand for a service may arise from patients or doctors.
Patients perceive that they need a service and hence demand it, although
the service may not be able to provide effective treatment for that need.
Demand in excess of actual need may originate from patients, doctors or
from quite different sources, such as pharmaceutical industry (Barker *et al.*
1998).

Contributions to the definitions of 'need' come from the fields of sociology, epidemiology, health economics and public health, as well as from
clinicians. Bradshaw (1972) outlined a 'taxonomy of social need'. This
distinguished between felt need (what people want), expressed need (felt
need turned into action), normative need (as defined by experts or professionals) and comparative need (arising where similar populations receive
different service levels). Raised within these distinctions are the questions
of: who determines need (professional, politician or public); what are
the influences of education and media in raising awareness about health
problems; and what are the cultural effects on need (Box 2.1). Social and
cultural factors have an enormous impact on levels of morbidity and on
health and the expression of health needs (Box 2.2).

Assessing need has an important practical use. The aim of any *needs
assessment* is to determine the level of problems and appropriate services
in a community, so that services can be planned accordingly. To aid this
approach, the pragmatic definition that 'need is the ability to benefit from

Box 2.1 Need: who decides and how?

Need can be:

- What an individual feels they want (felt need)
- What an individual demands (expressed need)
- What a professional thinks an individual wants (normative need)
- How we compare with others areas or situations (comparative need)

health care', originally developed by the NHS executive in the UK, is used in several countries. Needs assessment assumes that need, demand and supply do not currently overlap—there are instances when services are supplied that are not needed or demanded, and similarly there is need that is not being met (Fig. 2.1). The aim of conducting the needs assessment is to make need, demand and supply more closely match. Note that Fig. 2.1 suggests that need, demand, and supply are of equal size. There is little evidence to suggest that this is actually the case in many countries.

To estimate the need for palliative care two strategies may be adopted: epidemiological methods or current use of health services (Franks 1999). The epidemiological approach uses the cause-specific mortality in diseases which are likely to benefit from palliative care services, and then relates this to the type and frequency of symptoms experienced by patients suffering from these diseases (Franks 1999). It then reviews the effectiveness of care

Box 2.2 What influences need?

- Knowledge of what might be available and possible – influenced by friends, family, culture, media, internet, health professionals, etc
- Developments in knowledge
- Expectations from services in general
- Information about what works
- Ability to express the need – some people are more able to express needs than others
- Effect of peers and information on professionals
- What can be described and measured

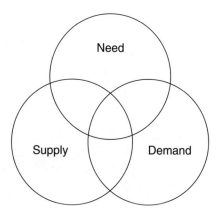

Fig. 2.1 Need, demand and supply do not completely overlap.

using international, national and local evidence. Health service use assesses need by identifying patients who are within the services. The limitation of this method is that it does not assess unmet need that must then be evaluated by alternative means (Franks 1999). This chapter will concentrate on the epidemiological approach to needs assessment in palliative day care.

Epidemiologically based needs assessment for palliative and terminal care

There has been considerable expansion in the provision of palliative care services in the last 30 years (Bosanquet 1999). The development of palliative care started in the late 1960s and was generally provided by non-specialists in hospitals, general practice and community nursing. In the 1970s and 1980s the main emphasis was on development of specialist services, first inpatient and day hospices then home care and then hospitals. The NHS reforms have put pressure on many hospices to define their services (Malson *et al.* 1996). By the 1990s there were new and growing concerns about access, quality and the organisation of these services (Bosanquet 1997). However, there are few robust results or established findings to guide decisions about management of palliative care services (Franks 1999).

In an attempt to provide assistance for those purchasing palliative care services, an epidemiologically-based needs assessment for palliative and terminal care was produced for the NHS Executive using the approach

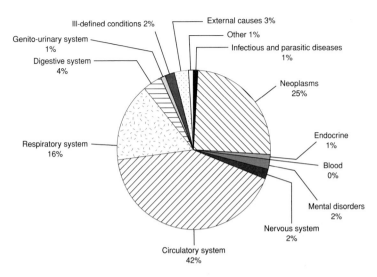

Fig. 2.2 Main causes of death, UK 1997, as classified by death registrations. N=570,000.

in Fig. 2.1 (Higginson 1997). The document provided standard definitions of palliative and terminal care and used national and local data on the incidence and prevalence of cancer and likely symptoms to estimate the numbers of patients and families needing palliative care. The numbers of patients dying from cancer and other diseases in a locality in the UK are available from the Office of National Statistics (ONS), local health authorities or primary care trusts.

Incidence and prevalence

The incidence of patients needing palliative care (either general and/or specialist input) can be estimated from death rates of common conditions which may require palliative care. In the United Kingdom there are about 570 000 deaths per year, most commonly from circulatory disorders, cancer and respiratory disease (Fig. 2.2). There are almost equal numbers of men and women who die, the numbers remain relatively constant over the time. A typical age distribution at death for the United Kingdom would be: <15 years, <1%; 16–35 years, 3%; 36–64 years, 19%; 65–74 years, 21%; 75+ years, 56%.

Clearly, the illness trajectory varies between diseases and not everybody will need specialist palliative care. However, many patients die from chronic or slowly progressive conditions who could benefit from palliative care. There are probably four main categories:

(1) Those whose illness progresses over time and who have symptoms that would benefit from intervention by a specialist palliative care service.

(2) Those who are relatively well, and suddenly deteriorate or die.

(3) Those whose illness is characterized by relapses and remissions and gradual deterioration over time.

(4) Those who wish for aggressive treatment aimed at cure, and resuscitation, whatever the likely benefit.

Those patients and families in Groups 1 and 3 are likely to need palliative care services and those in Groups 2 and 4 do not, although they will need symptom management and their families and friends may well need support. Applying the likely prevalence of symptoms for different conditions to the number of people who die can provide a closer estimate of need, although it will not take into account individual wants and preferences. For example, within a population of 100 000 people (eg. a primary care trust) national estimates suggest that there are approximately 280 cancer deaths per year, many of whom would have a period of advancing progressive disease, when palliative care would be appropriate. The estimates of prevalence of symptoms and problems are based on population- and other studies of patients with advanced disease and their families. Applying the population estimates to the 280 patients who would die from cancer a year suggests that there would be 230 with pain, 130 with breathlessness, 140 with vomiting or feeling sick, 200 with loss of appetite, and 90 where the patient had severe anxiety or worries and 70 where the family had severe anxiety or worries (Table 2.1).

It is possible to estimate the prevalence of symptoms and other problems in people with conditons other than cancer in the last year of life (Table 2.2). The number of people affected would be more than double that for cancer. Primary care plays an important role in the care of these patients and their families. For many conditions prognosis can be more uncertain than for cancers for which survival and mortality are well documented. These conditions may sometimes be acute, sometimes progressive and sometimes chronic, hence there will be a mix of patients falling into the four groups described above.

Traditionally, specialist palliative care services have concentrated on people with cancer, but this is changing. Such services see their role as increasingly providing expert symptom control and psychosocial advice

Table 2.1 Cancer patients: likely prevalence of problems (per 100 000 population).

Symptom	% with symptom in last year of life*	Estimated number in each year
Pain	84	240
Trouble with breathing	47	130
Vomiting or feeling sick	51	140
Sleeplessness	51	140
Mental confusion	33	90
Depression	38	110
Loss of appetite	71	200
Constipation	47	130
Bedsores	28	80
Loss of bladder control	37	100
Loss of bowel control	25	70
Unpleasant smell	19	50
Severe family anxiety/worries	33	90
Severe patient anxiety/worries	25	70
Total deaths from cancer		280

* As per Cartwright (1991) and Seale (1991) studies, based on a random sample of deaths and using the reports of bereaved carers.

* Anxiety as per Field et al. 1995 , Bennett et al. (1994) , Higginson et al. (1992), Addington Hall et al. (1991).

Note: Patients usually have several symptoms.

and care for people with other illnesses, in those instances where they have the skills to help.

Needs assessment and palliative day care

At the moment there is no good evidence to answer the question of how many of those patients with symptoms and problems 'need' day care. Current data suggest that the reasons for referral to day care include social interaction, respite for carer, psychological support, monitoring, symptom control, and assessment (Copp *et al.* 1998; Higginson *et al.* 2000a). It is suggested that palliative day care is suitable for patients who are not

Table 2.2 Patients with non-cancer progressive illness: likely prevalence of problems (per 100 000 population).

Symptom	% with symptom in last year of life*	Estimated number in each year
Pain	67	460
Trouble with breathing	49	340
Vomiting or feeling sick	27	180
Sleeplessness	36	250
Mental confusion	38	260
Depression	36	250
Loss of appetite	38	260
Constipation	32	220
Bedsores	14	100
Loss of bladder control	33	230
Loss of bowel control	22	150
Unpleasant smell	13	90
Severe family anxiety/worries	33	220
Severe patient anxiety/worries	25	160
Total deaths from other causes, excluding accidents, injury and suicide, and causes very unlikely to have a palliative period		680

* As per Cartwright (1991) and Seale (1991) studies, based on a random sample of deaths and using the reports of bereaved carers.

* Anxiety as per Field *et al.* 1995 , Bennett and Corcoran (1994) , Higginson *et al.* (1992), Addington Hall et al. (1991).

Note: Patients usually have several symptoms.

actively dying, but who have diminished ability to fulfil family and societal roles (Spencer and Daniels 1998).

Two surveys of palliative day care in the UK have increased our understanding of the objectives of day care, from the health professionals' perspective (Copp *et al.* 1998; Higginson *et al.* 2000a). Copp *et al.* undertook a telephone survey using a random sample of 131 day centres from 17 regional locations, providing 60% representation. Higginson *et al.* surveyed all 43 palliative day centres one health region (Thames) in order to understand how the types of interventions and goals of the services 'fit' within the pattern of palliative day care. The results from the both of the surveys suggest that:

◆ Most centres provide monitoring and review of symptoms/needs, bathing, wound care, physiotherapy, hairdressing, and aromatherapy.

◆ Different centres offer a variation of additional activities, including medical assessment, nurse-led clinic, art/music therapy, and trips.

◆ Symptoms regularly encountered by staff are pain, nausea and constipation (alone or in combination).

◆ Benefits to the patient and family include respite, companionship, support, monitoring of care, empowerment, and symptom control.

The range of medical and other psychosocial services appeared to be related to the source of funding for individual centres. Independently funded centres did not offer such a wide range of services as those that were part or wholly NHS-funded (Higginson *et al.* 2000a).

In 1999, data from the Hospice Information Service indicated that 10 000 places were available per week at over 230 day care centres in the UK (Jackson and Eve 1999). Most of the patient population utilising palliative day care had a cancer diagnosis. Many units were open to treating HIV/AIDS and motor neurone diesease (MND), but only 2% treated HIV and only 1% treated MND (Copp *et al.* 1998). The most frequent age range at many of the centres was 61–80 years, very few were under 40 years, and the higher ages (80+) were also less frequent. The total number of patients cared for each year was almost three times the number of new referrals, indicating that patients remain in day care for some time (Higginson *et al.* 2000a).

From these surveys it is still unclear how many people want day care (demand) or how many of those would benefit from it (need); no research studies exist that define the needs of the patients.

Effectiveness of palliative day care

A review of five systematic reviews of palliative care services could find no evaluation of the effectiveness of day care (Hearn and Higginson 1998; Salisbury *et al.* 1999; Smeenk *et al.* 1998; Rinck *et al.* 1997; Higginson *et al.* 2000b). One study from the US evaluated 'day hospital' as an alternative to in-patient care for cancer patients receiving chemotherapy (Mor *et al.* 1988a). This was part of the larger National Hospice Study

(Mor *et al.* 1988b). The results suggested no statistically significant differences between day hospital and in-patient care for medical or psychosocial outcomes. There were major differences in medical costs, which were approximately one-third lower for day hospital patients ($p < 0.001$) than for the in-patient group. However, there is little comparison between a US day hospital setting that was providing chemotherapy and other long-term intravenous treatment, and that provided by UK palliative day centres.

Conclusion

In the past, palliative care services were developed largely based on assumptions about patient need from the health professionals' points of view. Palliative care services are now having to adapt to changing demands upon them consequent upon changing patterns of disease (Higginson 1997), and the introduction of new therapies (Franks 1999), and ultimately to the challenge of providing care for patients with other chronic conditions. Assessment of the palliative care needs of the whole population is therefore essential for need, supply and demand to overlap.

Epidemiological data and analysis of existing health services can inform needs assessment. Currently little evidence exists about need from a patients perspective. It is imperative that patients' and carers' perspectives on need are sought and acted on if palliative care services are to adapt successfully to meet unmet need.

Summary Points

- In the UK health service need is defined as the ability to benefit from health care.
- Need can be defined from many perspectives and influenced by a range of factors.
- The purpose of needs assessment is to determine the levels of need and of existing service provision within the community in order to facilitate the planning of future services.
- The incidence and prevalence of symptoms, diseases and the causes of death can be used to provide an epidemiological basis of needs assessment.
- The objectives of palliative day care are increasingly being described, but at present there is a lack of information about which patients with

which kinds of 'need' need this type of care, and how effectively these needs are being met.

◆ Further research from the patients' perspective is required to assess need for palliative day care.

References

Addington-Hall, J. M., MacDonald, L., Anderson, H. and Freeling, P. (1991). Dying from cancer: the views of bereaved family and the friends about the experiences of terminally ill patients. *Palliative Medicine,* 5, 207–14.

Barker, D. J. P., Cooper, C. and Rose, G. (1998). *Epidemiology in medical practice.* Churchill Livingstone, London.

Bennett, M. and Corcoran, G. (1994). The impact on community palliative care services of a hospital palliative care team. *Palliative Medicine,* 8, 237–44.

Bosanquet, N. (1997). New challenge for palliative care. *British Medical Journal,* 314, 1294.

Bosanquet, N. (1999). Background and patterns of use of service. In *Providing a palliative care service: towards an evidence base,* (ed. N. Bosanquet and C. Salisbury, pp.8–10, 33–42. Oxford University Press, Oxford.

Bradshaw, J. S. (1972). A taxonomy of social need. In *Problems and progress in medical care: essays on current research,* (ed. McLachlan G.), pp. 71–82. Oxford University Press, Oxford.

Cartwright, A. (1991). Changes in life and care in the year before death 1969–1987. *Journal of Public Health Medicine,* 13, 81–7.

Copp, G., Richardson, A., McDaid, P. and Marshall-Searson, D. A. (1998). A telephone survey of the provision of palliative day care services. *Palliative Medicine,* 12, 161–70.

Field, D., Douglas, C., Jagger, C. and Dand, P. (1995). Terminal illness: views of patients and their lay carers. *Palliative Medicine,* 9, 45–54.

Franks, P. J. Question 2, need for palliative care. In *Providing a palliative care service: towards an evidence base,* (ed. N. Bosanquet and C. Salisbury), pp. 43–56. Oxford University Press, Oxford.

Hearn, J. and Higginson, I. J. (1998). Do specialist palliative care teams improve outcomes for cancer patients? A systematic literature review. *Palliative Medicine,* 12, 317–32.

Higginson, I. J. (1997). Chapter 4: palliative and terminal care. In *Health Care Needs Assessment: the epidemiologically based needs assessment reviews,* (ed. A. Stevens and J.Raftery), pp. 183–260. Wessex Institute of Public Health Medicine, Oxford.

Higginson, I. J., Wade, A. M. and McCarthy, M. (1992). Effectiveness of two palliative support teams. *Journal of Public Health Medicine,* 14, 50–6.

Higginson, I. J., Hearn, J., Myers, K. and Naysmith, A. (2000). What do palliative day centres do? *Palliative Medicine,*14, 277–86.

Higginson, I. J., Finlay, I., Goodwin, D. M., Cook, A. M. , Edwards, A. G. K., Hood. K. et al. (2000). *Evaluation of effectiveness and cost-effectiveness of palliative care teams—a systematic review.* Wales Office for Research and Development (WORD), Cardiff.

Jackson, A. and Eve, A. (1999). *The Hospice Information Service at St Christopher's. Directory 1999, Hospice and Palliative Care Services in the United Kingdom and Republic of Ireland.* Hospice Information Service, St Christopher's Hospice, London.

Malson, H., Clark, D., Small, N. and Mallett, K. (1996). The impact of NHS reforms on UK palliative care services. *European Journal of Palliative Care, 3,* 68–71.

Mor, V., Stalker, M. Z., Gralla, R., Scher, H. I., Cimma, C., Park, D. *et al.* (1988a). Day hospital as an alternative to inpatient care for cancer patients: a random assignment trial. *Journal of Clinical Epidemiology, 41,* 771–85.

Mor, V., Greer, D. S. and Kastenbaum, R. (1988b). *The hospice experiment.* The John Hopkins Press, Baltimore.

Rinck, G.C., van den Bos, G. A. M., Kleijnen, J., de Haes, H. J., Schade. E. and Veenhof, C. H. N. (1997). Methodological issues in effectiveness research on palliative cancer care: a systematic review. *Journal of Clinical Oncology, 15,* 1697–707.

Salisbury, C., Bosanquet, N., Wilkinson, E. K., Franks, P. J., Kite S., Lorentzon, M. *et al.* (1999).The impact of different models of specialist palliative care on patient's quality of life: a systematic literature review. *Palliative Medicine, 13,* 3–17.

Seale, C. (1992). A comparison of hospice and conventional care. *Social Science Medicine 32,* 147–52.

Smeenk, F. W. J. M., Van Haastregt J. C., M., De Witte, L. P. and Crebolder, F. J. M. (1998). Effectiveness of home care programmes for patients with incurable cancer on their quality of life: a systematic review. *British Medical Journal, 316,* 1939–43.

Spencer, D. J. and Daniels, L. E. (1998). Day hospice care—a review of the literature. *Palliative Medicine, 12,* 219–29.

3

Working across cultures of difference: ethnicity and the challenge for palliative day care

Yasmin Gunaratnam

Concerns about cultural sensitivity and race equality in palliative care appear to be fairly recent. However, it is important to recognise that a commitment to equitable service provision was very much a part of the foundations of palliative care. A statement of a commitment to race equality can be found within a 'Statement of Aims' of the 'Foundation Group' of St Christopher's Hospice as early as 1961, which stated that in hospice care there would be 'no barriers of race, colour or creed' (Melville 1990).

Despite this radical commitment to race equality at the beginning of the modern hospice movement, there have been growing concerns both in Britain (Field *et al.* 1997; Haroon-Iqbal *et al.* 1995; Hill and Penso 1995; O'Neill 1994) and in other countries (Brenner 1997; McNamara *et al.* 1997; Waddell and McNamara 1997) that hospice and palliative care is failing to meet the needs of people from a diversity of ethnic groups. Recommendations for improving service provision have included the need for service providers to collect different types of data on ethnicity (Smaje and Field 1997), the need for the recruitment of palliative care staff from a more diverse range of ethnic backgrounds (Hill and Penso 1995), the increased use of professional interpreters and advocates (Spruyt 1999), and specific training and education for professionals in inter-cultural care (McNamara *et al.* 1997).

All of these issues raise significant challenges for palliative day care which has been seen as focusing 'on the quality of life by attending to the physical, psychological, emotional, social and spiritual needs of patients and their families' (Fisher and McDaid 1996, p.5). Furthermore, despite increasing calls for attention to the evaluation of palliative day care provision (Copp *et al.* 1998; Spencer and Daniels 1998), a review of the literature revealed no specific work that had either addressed the experiences of service users from different ethnic groups or that had examined services with regard to issues of cultural sensitivity and race equality. This gap in the literature is perhaps more surprising in view of the report 'Opening Doors' by the National Council for Hospice and Specialist Palliative Care Services (NCHSPCS) that saw day care as playing a specific role in supporting 'black and Asian' service users and recommended an increase in day care services 'to meet the preferred needs of black and Asian patients' (Hill and Penso 1995, p.7).

In addressing this gap in the literature, this chapter will draw upon my qualitative research in a London Hospice. The study used multiple methods, combining one-to-one interviews with 23 service users from a range of African-Caribbean (n=11), Asian (n=8) and African backgrounds (n=4); 14 group interviews with 38 members[1] of hospice staff (the groups were predominantly white, British and female); participant observation in the hospice day centre and observation of two hospice home care teams.

The ethnographic and exploratory nature of the study means that the data are best interpreted as highlighting the specific context in which accounts have been produced rather than being used to draw precise generalisations from the study samples to wider populations. In drawing attention to the detail and meaning of lived experiences of ethnicity, the data can be valuable in informing service developments in day care.

Within this context, the chapter has two main aims: to provide an overview of research on ethnicity that has implications for day care; and to draw upon the accounts of hospice service users in the study to look at more complex ways of approaching issues of ethnicity and equity in service provision. Most significantly, I suggest that although ethnic identity can have an important influence on the needs of service users, the relationship between the two is more complex and multi-dimensional than current approaches to multi-cultural service development would suggest.

---

1. Five of these groups were part of a series of discussions held with the same social workers over a 12 month period.

Ethnicity and service use

Although there has been no specific research that has looked at ethnicity and day care provision, there are a number of findings from more general studies that can be used to inform our understanding of the current situation in Britain. The few published data suggest that ethnicity is related to the pattern of palliative care service use (Hill and Penso 1995; McNamara *et al.* 1997). The only national survey of hospice and specialist palliative care services to examine ethnicity for the first time in the year 1994–1995 (Eve *et al.* 1997) suggested that a higher percentage of 'non-white' service users (categorised using the 1991 census categories Black, Indian, Chinese and Other) received home care (3.1%) than were admitted to in-patients units (1.6%), with 2.1% receiving day care services.

Despite limited data from study sites in Brent, Newham and Birmingham health authorities, the 'Opening Doors' report stated that '. . . black and Asian patients generally prefer home care services supported by access to day care facilities' (Hill and Penso 1995, p.14). However, a study of the place of death of people with cancer in England between 1985–1994 suggests that there might be ethnicity-related differences with regard to actual place of death, with higher proportions of 'ethnic minority' service users with cancer dying in hospitals (Hearn 1997). The study has thus drawn attention to ethnicity-related inequalities in possible differences between preferences for care and choices about place of death.

A difficulty with both the national survey and the NCHSPCS study is that not only were both limited by an inadequate recording of the ethnicity of service users, but that they were also unable to address differences in service use between and within different ethnic groups or to determine the nature of such differences. However, more small scale, emerging research is beginning to overcome these particular limitations. Research on community-based palliative care to Bangladeshi people in Tower Hamlets in East London (Spruyt 1999) indicates that while there might be important ethnic, cultural and religious differences that need to be taken into consideration in looking at service use, the organisational 'culture' of services is also a part of the dynamic of service use.

In qualitative interviews with the bereaved primary carers of 18 people referred to a community palliative care team, four service users were said to have returned to Bangladesh to die. Of the remaining 14 service users, 10 had died at home, prompting Spruyt to comment: '. . . it is likely that differing ethnic groups will strongly favour home deaths because of their isolation in hospitals from poor communication, the differing food requirements and the desire to observe religious duties. Family members may also see it as a sacred duty to look after the patient themselves.' (Spruyt 1999, p.127). Other factors identified as affecting service use in the study were: low levels of fluency and literacy in English; little use of professional interpreters; and the exclusion of women carers in interpreted discussions. With regard to these findings, Spruyt has argued that: 'At the time of the study, there was no organisational commitment to addressing such issues and the pre-existing model of palliative care was applied to all regardless of ethnic background.' (Spruyt 1999, p. 127)

Despite the limitations of the data on ethnicity and service use, all of the findings from the different studies point to the need for service providers to identify and examine the relationships between the ethnic composition of their localities and differences in service use. Furthermore, emerging qualitative research, such as the study by Spruyt (1999) also suggests that such differences are not simply the result of ethnic and culturally related preferences, but can also be indicative of processes of discrimination that can be actively reinforced and produced through the operation of existing organisational policies and practices within palliative care.

Ethnicity and under-utilisation

Another theme in the literature on ethnicity and palliative care relates to concerns about the lower utilisation of services by different ethnic groups (Hill and Penso 1995; O'Neill 1994; Rees 1986). Two factors that are seen as having an effect upon utilisation rates are the relatively lower incidence of cancer within African-Caribbean, south Asian and African populations (Balarajan and Bulusu 1990; Balarajan and Raleigh 1993), and the fact that the incidence of deaths from cancer increases with age, occurring mainly in people over 55.

The much younger age structure of these groups in comparison to white, British populations (OPCS, 1993) and the emerging suggestion that many older black and Asian people 'emigrate back to their country of origin in later life' (Hill and Penso 1995, p.15), have been seen as possible explanations for the perceived low take-up of services. However, in a wider review of the literature on 'black and minority ethnic' people and cancer,[2]

---

2. Smaje and Field (1997) examined cancer data using both the 1991 census categories of ethnicity and data based upon 'place of birth'. In this latter category 'black and minority ethnic' populations were defined by the categories, Indian subcontinent, Caribbean Commonwealth and African Commonwealth.

Smaje and Field have suggested that: '. . . both the young age structure and the low incidence of cancer independently from age structure . . . are such that we would expect a lower need for palliative care. When the relatively small size of the these groups is also taken into consideration, it *may* be the case that there is no under-utilisation . . . and that low utilisation rates reflect genuinely lower levels of need. However, the data to hand do not allow us to do anything other than suggest this is a possibility . . . (Smaje and Field 1997, p.152, emphasis in original).

While it does appear that there may be no significant under-utilisation of services at present, the number of people over 55 from black and Asian groups is going to increase in the next decade (Hill and Penso 1995; Bahl 1996). It is highly likely, therefore, that the incidence of cancer within these groups is set to rise, leading to an increase in need for cancer related palliative care amongst these groups.

Palliative care for all

In addition to expected changes in need for palliative care among different ethnic groups, policy developments have also extended traditional approaches to need and are therefore also likely to influence the future ethnic composition of those defined in need of palliative care. A particularly significant development is the NHS Executive's clear requirement of 'Palliative Care for All' (EL(96)85; NHS Executive 1996), with the guidance recommending that: 'Purchasers of palliative care will wish to ensure that patients have *access* to *appropriate* palliative care services' (emphasis added).

Guidance produced by the NCHSPCS (Glickman 1997), covering the quality standards implications of EL(96)85, elaborated upon this focus, making clear that issues of equity, acceptability, accessibility and appropriateness were to be central themes in the development of quality assurance standards within service provision. The guidance drew attention to both employment practices and service user experiences relating to culture, religion and language for specific consideration in service development: 'Setting formal standards is an opportunity to promote equal opportunities in employment and personnel practices, access to services and treatment of patients/carers. Standards should recognise diversity of religion, culture and language in the populations served.' (p. 20).

Alongside these policy developments, there has been a growing recognition both within palliative care (Doyle 1993; Addington-Hall *et al.* 1998; McCarthy *et al.* 1996) and the wider health service (National

Association of Health Authorities and Trusts 1991) for palliative care to meet the needs of people with non-malignant diseases, often referred to as the 'disadvantaged dying'. This broadening of access to palliative care has specific implications for the ethnic mix of potential service users. In a study of ethnicity and specialist palliative care services in the city of Derby over a 12 month period, Fountain (1999) has argued that the small number of referrals from 'ethnic minorities' (1.5%) has specific implications for the future of palliative care provision. Since the findings from the study attributed low utilisation rates primarily to epidemiology, Fountain has argued that: '... ethnic minorities have a very different pattern of mortality, being more likely than white patients to die of coronary heart disease and strokes ... Specialist palliative care ... for patients with cardiac disease in the UK is currently negligible. If palliative care is to be freely available to ethnic minorities, we may need to be more flexible about seeing patients with a non-malignant diagnosis.' (Fountain 1999, p.162).

Taken together, these various factors (relating to current and future service use, policy developments within palliative care and epidemiology) suggest that day care services have the potential to play a significant role in meeting the current and future needs of service users from a diversity of ethnic groups. Although this role will have particular implications for those services in areas with relatively large numbers of people from different ethnic backgrounds, a concern with equity in service provision can also enhance quality of care for all service users. In this sense, what is important is the process of service development that is involved in addressing diversity. Such a process can enable more complex ways of addressing need, administering care, training and supporting staff and evaluating service provision that has something to offer all service providers and users.

Ethnicity, equity and need

Issues relating to the need for palliative care are central to discussions about equitable service provision since they have implications for methods of addressing service accessibility, utilisation, demand and supply. However, the majority of studies that have examined these factors have been based upon quantitative research, without eliciting the views of service users about their perceptions and experiences of illness and of services (Hill and Penso 1995; Rees 1986). Such an omission is highly significant in considering the philosophy of holistic care, which as Clark and Seymour

(1999) have pointed out extends and complicates traditional concepts of 'need', based largely upon the physical needs of individuals: 'Palliative care of course seeks to look beyond physical needs, so the question of emotional and social needs is also introduced. Likewise the focus of care may go beyond the patient, to include the needs of informal carers. In such a way the assessment of palliative care needs starts to become a rather complex matrix .' (Clark and Seymour 1999, p.143).

The predominance of quantitative approaches to need presents specific problems in addressing the service needs of different ethnic groups, particularly when considering emotional and social factors. For example, Fig. 3.1 represents a 'conventional' model for examining ethnicity and service need in which population characteristics based upon ethnic categories, other demographic characteristics, disease specific mortality rates and expected deaths can be used to assess need and along with service utilisation data can also be used to examine access to services.

At a basic level, the need for palliative care can be addressed by considering variations in the demographic and epidemiological profiles of

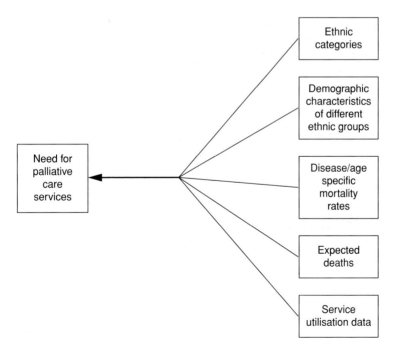

Fig. 3.1 A traditional model for examining service need.

different groups and how these relate to the rates for specific diseases and conditions (Smaje and Field 1997). The interpretation of such data are far from straightforward however. For example, in my own research I found a range of psychosocial factors in service user accounts that could be seen as having an effect upon need and service use, and which also suggest that relationships between ethnicity and service need are far from straightforward. Some of these factors are represented as the 'hidden' intervening variables in Fig. 3.2.

The significance of these and other 'hidden' factors are also relevant for how we interpret quantitative data. For instance, while lower than expected utilisation rates may indicate an inaccessibility of services to particular groups they may also reflect the existence of particular attitudes towards health and service provision which are not simply related to the accessibility of services.

Similarly, expected or even higher utilisation rates do not necessarily represent an equitable service or the meeting of needs, particularly when much of the data on ethnicity used to calculate rates is based upon those born abroad and may not be suitable for wider application to those who have been born or brought up in the UK (Smaje and Field 1997). It is also the case that the reliability of the recording of ethnicity by hospice and palliative care services has been questioned (Hill and Peso 1995;

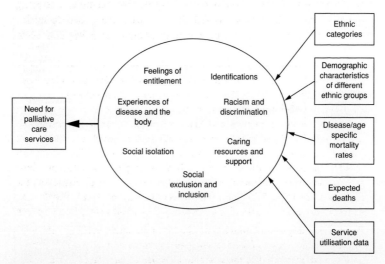

Fig. 3.2 A new model for examining service need showing psychosocial factors.

A. Eve, personal communication 1999) and may be subject to recording biases[3] that could affect estimates of need.

Data from more general research is useful in unravelling some of these issues further. Smaje and Le Grand (1997) in an examination of the use of general practitioner, outpatient and inpatient services by 'black and minority ethnic' people suggested that with the exception of Chinese people[4] 'there is no gross pattern of inequity in the use of health services by different ethnic groups in Britain' (Smaje and Le Grand 1997, p.493). However, despite the lack of conclusive statistical evidence of significant patterns of inequality, the authors point to several psychosocial factors as mediating the interpretation of their data. These factors included:

- differences in lay beliefs about health and illness amongst Chinese people and their possible influences upon pathways between biomedical and 'traditional' care;

- the possibility that 'over-utilisation' of particular services could reflect poorer experiences in the quality of services;

- the lack of understanding of the relationships between self-reported health status and 'need' for services amongst 'black and minority ethnic' people.

Such issues point to some of the difficulties in using quantitative data alone to examine issues of ethnicity and equity. For example, a growing number of researchers have argued that the categories used to define ethnicity are both flawed and problematic (Ahmad and Sheldon 1992;

---

3. An examination of data on ethnicity from a survey of hospice and palliative care services for the year 1997–1998, by the Hospice Information Service (A. Eve, personal communication 1999)has shown that where there was a recording of large numbers of people from black and Asian groups, there was also a correspondingly higher percentage of cases where ethnicity was recorded as 'not known'. It has been suggested that this could mean that ethnicity is recorded more diligently where there are relatively large numbers of people from different ethnic groups. However, such variations in recording practices further supports the findings of the NCHSPCS report (Hill an Penso 1995) that within hospice and palliative care, ethnic monitoring 'is not being approached systematically' (p. 15).

4. People who categorised themselves as Chinese in the study were found to have a much lower utilisation of services compared to other ethnic groups. The categories of ethnicity used in the study were: White, Indian, East African, Asian, Pakistani, Bangladeshi, Chinese, Caribbean, African, Mixed Origin, None of these.

Benezeval *et al.* 1995; Husband 1982). At one level, there is no denying the fact that ethnic categories have meaning and a 'symbolic logic' (Smaje 1996) both within everyday life and in service development. Such categories have provided a useful starting point in identifying and examining differences in service need and use. However, as Smaje (1996) argues: '. . . it is vital to recognise that the neat ethnic categories demanded by research (and typically assumed in everyday life) are partly fictional. Thus, insights derived from . . . research are best used to help formulate further questions about the social contexts within which both ethnicity and health experiences are framed.' (Smaje 1996, p.165).

It is also the case that equity is a multi-dimensional concept, and its various dimensions are not always congruent (Sen 1992). Thus, equality of access cannot in itself ensure equality of utilisation because of differences in service users' perceptions and experiences of need. Similarly, equality of opportunity may lead to inequalities in outcome because some individuals are 'better equipped than others to take advantage of the opportunities available' (Philips *et al.* 1994, p. 15). Yet it is precisely these important factors that can remain hidden within current models which have failed to address how lived experiences of ethnicity challenge traditional approaches to equity.

Hence it can become much more difficult to use and interpret measures of service need because of the interacting influences of social, cultural and subjective experiences that can affect all the relevant variables—that is the meaning given to ethnicity and experiences of health, illness and service provision. As such, issues of race equality can be seen to fall into the 'person regarding' rather than 'lot regarding' (Rae 1981) concepts of equity, which extend beyond issues of equal access, use, treatment and outcome, to include the recognition of *different* people being enabled to derive *equal* (rather than the *same*) value from the same services. In other words, traditional measures of need can lose their direct usefulness precisely because equitable service provision in response to difference can call for unequal treatment and therefore also unequal outcomes.

Lived experiences and the challenge for 'categorical' thinking

As I have pointed out, there are difficulties in addressing the need for palliative care among different ethnic groups, however both research and service development have also been limited by the lack of attention given to lived experiences of ethnicity. For example, in my study although there were commonalities of experience based upon ethnic identity, there were also variations based upon differences of gender, age, class, region religious/spiritual identity and experiences of disease and illness (Gunaratnam 2001a).

Important questions here are what implications do these issues have for the provision of day care services? And how can we begin to address these in our work with service users? As a starting point, there is much to be gained from examining the nature of existing multi-cultural approaches to service development and how these relate to the complexity of lived experience.

In general, ethnicity has been addressed in palliative care through a focus upon categories of national, cultural and religious identity (Green 1989, 1992; Neuberger 1987). This has led to multi-cultural service developments characterised by what I call 'categorical thinking' in which service provision has been based upon meeting particular expressions of 'need' within the different categories. Thus the NCHSPCS report (Hill and Penso 1995) defined culturally sensitive service provision primarily in terms of 'language, religion, spiritual and dietary needs' (p.5). While such provisions as multi-faith support or the availability of a variety of foods are very important, the process of addressing needs in this way can become tokenistic and at worst the opportunity to provide flexible, responsive and individual care can be easily missed (Gunaratnam 1997).

My argument is that although ethnic and cultural identifications can influence service needs, such identifications are in a constant process of movement, negotiation and production, in which experiences of disease can also have an effect upon cultural practices.[5] This can be illustrated with examples about food from my study. For some of the service users in the study, disease and its progression had led to changes in taste that affected choices about diet, with specific problems being identified with 'spicy' food. Other individuals had rejected their 'usual' diet as a part of a 'healthy-eating' approach developed in response to their illness, while others said that they positively enjoyed the opportunity to eat English food 'for a change' (Gunaratnam 2001a).

The complex effects of individual choice and disease and treatment on taste illustrate some of the difficulties in using traditional multi-cultural approaches which can be limiting not only for service providers but also for service users (Gunaratnam 2001b). Nasreen, a Ugandan service user,

---

5. For more detailed examples of how culturally related eating practices can be modified in relation to disease , see Gunaratnam 2001a, 2001b.

appeared concerned that changes in her preferences between 'African' and 'English' food options and her recent dislike of meat created extra work for staff while also wasting food. She worried that: 'they might cook it and I won't like it and it's a waste . . . like now I refuse meat, even chicken, I eat and I just throw up'.

Hunt (1996) has described how disease can lead to changes in experiences of taste, the smell of food, and how even the colour of particular foods or 'the large expanse of colour on a plate' may affect what is perceived as appetising. Hunt recommends that day care staff need to examine food preferences amongst service users at frequent and short intervals. However it is apparent that service users from different ethnic groups may also need specific support in addressing how changes in disease and in treatment may affect their taste and necessitate modifications to their diet. Such support may also enable individuals to reframe their experiences as a common part of the disease process, rather than being seen as creating extraordinary 'problems' for services.

I have used the example of food to look at some of the limitations of traditional multi-cultural approaches; however, the process underlying my analysis can also be useful in countering more general tendencies to stereotype the needs of service users from different ethnic groups. As such, I would suggest that it is productive for service providers and staff to approach service development in day care by first familiarising themselves with the nature of dominant definitions and categories of local need and how these are expressed by local groups.

For example, in areas where there are large numbers of Pakistani, Muslim people, attention may be given initially to issues of language, religion and food in day care provision. However, the second important part of the process would involve bringing out and exploring actively the ways in which lived experiences of ethnicity and disease overflow the limits of these more general categories of ethnic/cultural/religious need and also draw attention to gaps in existing service provision and care.

Experiences of social exclusion

Although attention has been given to ethnic, cultural and religious identity in addressing service needs, for people from groups racialised as 'ethnic minorities' wider socio-economic conditions, such as experiences of social exclusion, isolation and poverty can also affect access to services, service needs, perceptions of quality of life and expectations of service provision. These experiences can affect people at a number of levels and have implications for both the range and the nature of the support that is made available to service users.

For example, a very practical issue concerns the accessibility of day care provision. Research has found that people from 'ethnic minority' groups tend to be highly concentrated in urban areas (Owen 1994; Modood *et al.* 1997). This residential concentration can also mean that people from particular groups have less access to employment, transport and good quality housing (Robinson 1989). A survey of hospice provision in the United States (Gordon 1996) has noted that concerns about the location of housing for African-American people was seen as an important issue by service providers in judgements about the accessibility of services for hospices with 'black' and Hispanic people in their areas.

In talking to day care service users in my study a significant theme in talk about experiences of day care related to the critical importance of day care in combating social isolation, with particular attention being given to the value of transport in enabling individuals to use the service. Talk about day care was thus often related to social context, including references to family support and social isolation. Hilda, a Jamaican, retired hospital 'domestic', told me: '. . . they (the hospice) have tried to help me instead of leaving me at home to wander, sit in the house and wander around the four walls. They have helped me come into the centre and associate with other people. I mean it change my life style a whole lot because, had it not been that they take me up here twice per week, um, I wouldn't be able to get out as much as I'm doing because the boys (sons) are at work and (. . .) when they come in they might be tired and eventually it would only be weekend I'm able to go out, but at the moment now I comes out twice per week which is a great help and support for me. I gain strength. I come to the Centre I meet other people, I make friends and I share love, so it's a great support.'

In addition to what service users told me during interviews, I was also able to observe how individuals used the service and communicated with one another during my participant observation as a volunteer in the hospice day centre. These two forms of data suggest a more complex interaction of factors surrounding the role of day care in providing support to different service users. In ethnographic research in a palliative day care unit Langley-Evans and Payne (1997) have observed that the environment was characterised by a focus upon talking rather than simply the 'doing' of activities.

Langley-Evans and Payne have pointed to the particular therapeutic value of humorous talk about death, illness and cancer amongst service users. Although such findings were supported in my own research, I also found differences in service users' participation in day centre talk and activities. Of particular relevance here was the apparent threatening nature of talk to some individuals, that also appeared to be related to their non-participation in social interactions within the day centre.

Frank, a Jamaican man of 76, who had been a motor mechanic, described himself as 'a loner' and told me that in the day centre: 'I always like to sit on my own. I don't like too much talking, 'cause it irritate me and so on.' However in asking Frank about his choices, it also appeared that fear of antagonising others with different beliefs and attitudes also played a role in his non-participation in the centre: 'I'm a very quiet person. I don't like too many friends, so much company, 'cause they put you in trouble, and I stay in my own place, even I been up there (day centre) I could be in one place. I just relax until I feel all right . . . I don't like too much talking and sometimes you know . . . you might say something that go against you that you shouldn't say. You don't know . . . when I was in that pension club, before I took sick, I had a few friends there, white chaps . . . and I said to one of them about God . . . and they used to get very angry, very annoyed and say there is no such thing.' In drawing attention to differences between himself and the 'white chaps', inter-racial relations can also be seen as having relevance in contributing to the threatening nature of social interactions for some service users. It is also possible that past experiences of racism and social exclusion may have an effect upon the ability of some service users to take full advantage of the opportunities for social support offered by day care or to make demands upon the service.

Appropriate and sensitive service provision in this context will entail attention not simply to ethnic identity, but also to individual practices, and feelings about different aspects of day care services and to the broader biographical and social context in which such feelings have been generated. As Martha Nussbaum's (1995) work on 'human capabilities' has cautioned: 'The poor and deprived frequently adjust their expectations and aspirations to the low level of life they have known. Thus, they may not demand more education, better health care, (Nussbaum 1995, p.91). Addressing the effects of social inequalities in service use is thus complex and challenging, raising fundamental questions about how services can recognise and combat the effects of social exclusion while also enabling service users to make demands upon the service.

In my research, I often found it difficult to find out what individuals really wanted from services. Some people felt so privileged to be receiving services that they were anxious not be seen as 'complaining'. Others saw their needs as being 'extraordinary' and were therefore reluctant to make any demands upon services, even when the quality of some aspects of provision was perceived to be low. Such issues can be seen in the following extract from an interview with Mohammed, a Bangladeshi, Muslim service user, where he talks about his experiences of halal food as a hospice inpatient:

Yasmin: So do you eat halal food here?

Mohammed: Most of the time, it comes from, my wife bring it or my brother-in-law . . . Almost everyday . . . I don't have any problems about food.

Yasmin: But did you know that they provide halal food here? . . .

Mohammed: Yes.

Yasmin: And what did you think about it?

Mohammed: Er, it's, it's all right. I don't like to complain . . . so I don't want to say because they can't make it. They can't. Perhaps, I've been many times in the hospital, many hospital and I was in the trade . . . So I know it is going to be difficult . . . the problem is I don't know from where they get this food. It's not good at all . . . I don't make any complaint.

Yasmin: No. No I am just interested about how you could improve it really. How would you-?

Mohammed: Well if they, if they advertise they can get many, many people, they can supply . . . there are some shops in East London (. . .) but for 2 or 3 peoples they can't get it from East London . . . How many peoples are in here having halal eh?

Within this extract are a combination of issues which include a reluctance to be seen as criticising the service, the availability of wider social support and resources, a willingness to categorise personal needs as being 'difficult', and the effects of perceptions of the small numbers of other Muslim service users on feelings of entitlement. The variety of the issues raised provide some insight into how social inequalities can operate to link a diversity of social and psychosocial experiences, producing a range of potential practices and interactions that carry implications for how different individuals are positioned within particular service environments and how they might position *themselves* in relation to the service.

In this sense inequalities can be understood as being constructed at several different levels: by social conditions, their relation to organisational structures and activities and also how such interactions affect and give meaning to individual feelings, thoughts and actions. The contradictions here are that the strategies that individuals use to negotiate inadequacies in service provision can be the same strategies that both leave these inadequacies unchallenged *and* fail to enable the inclusion of service users' needs within 'mainstream' provision.

As Spencer and Daniels (1998) have pointed out, there can be gaps between the aims of day care providers and how individuals actually use the service. They therefore suggest that 'mechanisms are required to evaluate the extent to which day services meet the need of patients and the philosophical aims of the organization' (p.224).

Conclusion

In view of the complexity of representations of experiences of ethnicity, how can day care services provide an equitable and responsive service to people from a diversity of ethnic groups? Considering the limitations of current approaches to ethnicity in palliative care, there are three main issues that service providers need to engage with. These are: a move away from categorical thinking; a critical examination of the underlying ethos and culture of day care provision; and an exploration of the ways in which experiences of social inequalities and of exclusion may affect service relations.

As I have shown, categorical thinking has tended to characterise how ethnicity has been addressed in palliative care leading to a somewhat formulaic approach, in which service provision has been dominated by the categorising of need at the cost of service flexibility and responsiveness. This has meant that although some service providers have appeared to cater for differences in need, such provisions have not necessarily led to the inclusion of a diversity of experiences within the service, or to a fuller understanding of the complexity of lived experiences of ethnicity. Thus, although much multi-cultural provision is based upon the valuable recognition that a diversity of service choices are important in providing symbolic and practical support to service users, these same approaches can be based upon limiting conceptualisations of ethnicity.

Second, it is important for day care providers to recognise how their ability to respond fairly and sensitively to service needs also entails organisational scrutiny. In this sense issues of 'cultural difference' are best understood as being constructed in the relationship *between* the cultural identity of the organisation and that of the service user, rather than being seen as related solely to the identity of the service user. Such an approach suggests a more active role for multi-cultural service development, in which there is also a need for continuous critical evaluation of the nature of service provision and service user experiences.

This latter point has specific implications for a recognition of how wider social inequalities impact upon the service needs, expectations and practices of individuals from different ethnic groups. As I have argued, the availability of different multi-cultural provision, is not enough by itself to enable equitable service provision.

In this sense a consideration of ethnicity and social inequalities serves also to challenge and complicate models of individually tailored care, by highlighting the need to make links between the individual and the wider social, economic and historical context in which they live. This is perhaps the most important issue, requiring a creative tension between existing knowledge and awareness and an ever-ready willingness to know and to do 'differently' based upon the complex and changing experiences of service users.

Summary points

- Little, if any attention has been given to research on the experiences of service users from different ethnic groups in palliative day care. The paper presents findings from a qualitative study that included interviews with day care service users from African, African-Caribbean and South Asian backgrounds and participant observation in a hospice day centre.

- There is a need to move away from 'categorical' approaches to the service needs of people from different ethnic groups. Lived experiences of ethnicity, culture, religion and disease can affect service need and use, and these are diverse, unstable and changing.

- Issues of cultural difference are constructed in the dynamic relationship between the individual and the organisation. There is a need for continuous evaluation of the nature of service provision and service user experiences.

- Wider social inequalities affect the service needs, expectations and practices of individuals from different ethnic groups and should be addressed in service development.

References

Addington-Hall, J., Fakhoury, W. and McCarthy, M. (1998). Specialist palliative care in nonmalignant disease. *Palliative Medicine*, **12**, 417–427.

Ahmad, W. and Sheldon, T. (1993). 'Race' and statistics. In *Social Research, philosophy, politics and practice*, (ed. M. Hammersley), pp 124–130. Sage Publications in association with the Open University Press, London.

Bahl, V. (1996). Cancer and ethnic minorities the Department of Health's perspective. *British Journal of Cancer*, **74** (Suppl. XXIX), 2–10.

Balarajan, R. and Bulusu, L. (1990). Mortality among immigrants in England and Wales, 1979–83. In *Mortality and geography: a review in the mid-1980s*, (ed. M. Britton), pp 103–121. OPCS, London (Series DS No.9).

Balarajan, R. and Raleigh, V. (1993). *Health of the nation—ethnicity and health— a guide for the NHS*. Department of Health, London.

Benezeval, M., Judge, K. and Smaje, C. (1995). Beyond class, race and ethnicity: deprivation and health in Britain. *Health Services Research*, **30**, 163–177.

Brenner, P. (1997). Issues of access in a diverse society. *Hospice Journal*, **12**, 9–16.

Clark, D. and Seymour, J. (1999). *Reflections on palliative care*. Open University Press, Buckingham.

Copp, G., Richardson, A., McDaid, P. and Marshall-Searson, D.A. (1998). A telephone survey of the provision of palliative day care services. *Palliative Medicine*, **12**, 161–170.

Doyle, D. (1993). Specialist palliative care services defined. In *Needs assessment for hospice and specialist palliative care services: from philosophy to contracts*. (ed. M. Robbines), pp. 11–15. National Council for Hospice and Specialist Palliative Care Services, London.

Eve, A., Smith, A. and Tebbit, P. (1997). Hospice and palliative care in the UK 1994–5, including a summary of trends 1990–5. *Palliative Medicine*, **11**, 31–43.

Field, D., Hockey, J. and Small, N. (1997). *Death, gender and ethnicity*. Routledge, London.

Fisher, R.A. and McDaid, P. (1996). *Palliative day care*. Arnold, London.

Fountain, A. (1999). Ethnic minorities and palliative care in Derby. *Palliative Medicine*, **13**, 161–162.

Glickman, M. (1997). *Making palliative care better: quality improvement, multi-professional audit and standards*. Occasional Paper 12. National Council for Hospice and Specialist Palliative Care Services, London.

Gordon, A. (1996). Hospices and minorities: a national study of organisational access and practice. *Hospice Journal*, **11**, 49–70.

Green, J. (1989). *Death with dignity: meeting the spiritual needs of patients in a multi-cultural society*. Macmillan Magazines, London.

Green, J. (1992). *Death with dignity: meeting the spiritual needs of patients in a multi-cultural society, Vol. 2*. Macmillan Magazines, London.

Gunaratnam, Y. (1997). Culture is not enough: a critique of multi-culturalism in palliative care. In *Death, gender and ethnicity,* (ed. D. Field, J. Hockey and N. Small), pp 168–186. Routledge, London.

Gunaratnam, Y. (2001a). Ethnicity and palliative care. In *Sociology, ethnicity and nursing practice,* (ed. L. Culley and S. Dyson) pp 169–185. Macmillan, London.

Gunaratnam, Y. (2001b) . Eating into Multi-culturalism: Hospice staff and service users talk race, ethnicity, identity and food. *Critical Social Policy,* 21, 287–310.

Hill, D. and Penso, D. (1995). *Opening doors: improving access to hospice and specialist care services by members of black and ethnic minority communities.* National Council of Hospice and Specialist Palliative Care Services, London.

Haroon-Iqbal, H., Field, D. Parker, H. and Iqbal, Z. (1995) Palliative care services for ethnic groups in Leicester. *International Journal of Palliative Nursing,* 1, 114–116.

Hearn, J. (1997). Trends in the place of death of cancer patients over ten years: focus on patients born outside the UK. Unpublished Msc Dissertation. University of London.

Hunt, T. (1996). Nutritional needs. In *Palliative Day Care* (ed. R.A. Fisher and P. McDaid), pp. 169–177. Arnold, London.

Husband, C. (1982). Race *in Britain: continuity and change.* Hutchinson, London.

Langley-Evans, A. and Payne, S. (1997). Light-hearted death talk in a palliative day care context. *Journal of Advanced Nursing,* 26, 1091–1097.

McCarthy, M., Lay, M. and Addington-Hall, J. (1996). Dying from heart disease. *Journal of the Royal College of Physicians,* 30, 325–328.

McNamara, B., Martin, K., Wadell, C., and Yuen, K. (1997). Palliative care in a multi-cultural society: perceptions of health care professionals. *Palliative Medicine,* 11, 359–367.

Melville, J. (1990). *St Christopher's Hospice.* Together Publishing Company, London.

Modood, T., Berthoud, R., Lakey, J., Nazroo, J., Smith., P., Virdee, S. *et al.* (1997). *Ethnic minorities in Britain: diversity and disadvantage.* Policy Studies Institute, London.

National Association of Health Authorities and Trusts. (1991). *Care of people with terminal illness—a report by a joint advisory group.* National Association of Health Authorities and Trusts, Birmingham.

Neuberger, J. (1987). *Caring for dying people of different faiths.* Austen Cornish and Lisa Sainsbury Foundations, London.

NHS Executive. (1996). *A policy framework for commissioning cancer services,* EL(96)85. NHS Executive, Leeds.

Nussbaum, M. (1995). Human capabilities, female human beings. In *Women, culture and development* (ed. M. Nussbaum and J. Glover), pp 61–115. Oxford University Press, Oxford.

O'Neill, J. (1994). Ethnic minorities—neglected by palliative care providers? *Journal of Cancer Care*, **3**, 215–20.

OPCS (1993). Ethnic group and country of birth: Great Britain. 1991 Census. HMSO, London.

Owen, D. (1994). Spatial variations in ethnic minority group populations in Great Britain. *Population Trends*, **78**, 23–33.

Philips, C., Palfrey, C. and Thomas, P. (1994). *Evaluating health and social care.* MacMillan, Basingstoke.

Rae, D. (1981). *Equalities.* Harvard University Press, Cambridge, MA.

Rees, W.D. (1986). Immigrants and the hospice. *Health Trends*, **27**, 114–9

Robinson, V. (1989). Race, space and place: the geographical study of UK ethnic relations 1967–1987. *New Community*, **14**, 186–97.

Sen, A. (1992). *Inequality reexamined.* Oxford University Press, Oxford.

Smaje, C. (1996). The ethnic patterning of health: new directions for theory and research. *Sociology of Health and Illness*, **18**, 139–71.

Smaje, C. and Field, D. (1997). Absent minorities? Ethnicity and the use of palliative care services. In *Death, gender and ethnicity*, (ed. D. Field, J. Hockey and N. Small), pp. 142–65. Routledge, London.

Smaje, C. and Le Grand, J. (1997). Ethnicity, equity and the use of health services in the British NHS. *Social Science and Medicine*, **45**, 485–96.

Spencer, D.J. and Daniels, L.E. (1998). Day hospice care—a review of the literature. *Palliative Medicine*, **12**, 219–29.

Spruyt, O. (1999). Community-based palliative care for Bangladeshi patients in east London. Accounts of bereaved carers. *Palliative Medicine*, **13**, 119–29.

Waddell, C. and McNamara, B. (1997). The stereotypical fallacy: a comparison of Anglo and Chinese Australians' thoughts about facing death. *Mortality*, **2**, 149–161.

PART B. PROVIDING DAY CARE

4
_____

Establishing day care

Karon O'Keefe

The literature provides very little direction on how to plan and establish a palliative day care service. Most reports have focused on the needs assessment or quality improvement activities undertaken by established services. This chapter aims to raise awareness of issues that require consideration, and some of the policies, procedures and physical requirements when both establishing a new palliative day care service, and maintaining an ongoing service. The key issues are summarised in Box 4.1.

Needs assessment

The viability of a palliative day care service for the catchment area must be considered. Analysis of current service provision to the population must be carried out because some patients may well be able to access other services, such as luncheon or social clubs instead of, or as well as, palliative day care. These issues are discussed further in Chapter 2.

A review by Wiles *et al.* (1999) identified a number of elements that are necessary for evaluating the level at which services are already provided prior to implementing change or developing new services. The elements they identified were:

- a description of current services available;
- interviews with provider stakeholders;
- interviews with patients and carers;
- questionnaire survey of general practitioners and community nurses.

The information gathered prior to the planning of a new day centre service should assist in determining:

- the number of patients who may access a day centre service;
- the definitions of patient categories to whom care could be provided;

Box 4.1 Key issues for establishing palliative day care.

Needs assessment

◆ Determining the number and types of patients who may access the service.

Mapping out a service network

◆ Establishing current service provision and existing resources within the catchment area.

Referral criteria

◆ Establishing referral criteria based on local patient needs. Determine potential sources and routes for referral.

Service specifications

◆ Generating a framework by which the service delivery can be measured, including the means to reflect on current practice, and methods for evaluation and audit.

Policies

◆ Developing an operational policy in the light of patients' needs. This will define the reasons that particular services are required within the palliative day care service.

Marketing

◆ Planning for the launch of a new service by targeting local referrers and raising awareness. An ongoing plan will also be necessary to ensure continued use of the service.

Problems to avoid

◆ Establishing clear criteria and policies regarding admission, review and discharge of patients.

◆ Funding should be secured to ensure ongoing running of the service, as well as capital works.

◆ Planning should allow for administrative support and leave requirements for staff.

- the numbers of patients who may fall into each of the patient categories requiring care;
- the sources of referral to the service;
- possible patterns of service use;
- the effect of offering day care on the delivery of related community and inpatient services;
- other key stakeholders who may provide information and feedback throughout the process.

Mapping out a service network

Organisational and inter-organisational agency maps can be developed as a way of 'graphically illustrating and describing the agency's place in the service network and aspects of its operation' (Jackson and Donovan 1999). In the case of a palliative care day centre the relationships between services, departments and external agencies could be described. The information could be represented as a chart or may simply be described as a part of the planning process. The advantages of this process are:

- the mapping process itself often has the effect of increasing awareness of services due to its collaborative nature;
- it allows for a process where stakeholders can communicate and increase understanding of existing issues as well as possibly uncovering different perceptions;
- service anomalies can be revealed;
- similarities and differences can be analysed so that duplication is avoided (Jackson and Donovan 1999).

Referral criteria

It has been suggested that one of the problems facing purchasers is 'not simply whether individuals may benefit (from components of a specialist palliative care service) but *which* individuals with *which* categories of pathology (and social circumstance) should be provided with *which* general pattern of service' (Robbins 1993). The principle of deciding to whom it would be appropriate to offer palliative day care is important in establishing the service and clarifying the aims of care. Service providers need to address the issue of whether patients with some diagnoses will be excluded.

Types of patient who may benefit from day care should be defined as a result of needs assessment and the planning process. Suggested categories may include:

◆ patients needing basic treatment on an outpatient basis;

◆ patients needing respite care, i.e. those who live alone or with carers but who require time and activities in a different environment to enable them to continue living at home in the long term;

◆ patients who require allied health input in order to maintain their daily living activities in their own home, i.e. rehabilitation;

◆ patients who would benefit from the company of others and attention to their psychological and spiritual needs by skilled professionals.

Patients who require more intensive nursing and medical input or patients in the imminently terminal phase of their disease would not be appropriate. It is important to state clearly any exclusion criteria in the admission policy, because this will help guide referrers regarding the appropriateness of referral.

Service specification

The development of service specifications by purchasers of services has occurred over the past eight years. Service specifications aim to ensure that a framework is applied to agreements between purchasers and providers of care. The suggested content of a service specification has been defined in an Occasional Paper by the Trent Palliative Care Centre (Neale *et al.* 1993) and includes:

◆ definition of values and objectives underpinning service delivery;

◆ policy and management, reflecting current practice;

◆ research and development;

◆ level of service provision—as suggested earlier to ensure equitable access;

◆ training and education;

◆ direct care for service users;

◆ health promotion;

◆ multidisciplinary teams;

◆ communication and continuity of care;

◆ quality improvement strategies.

Although these areas may be agreed between the purchaser and the provider, an operational policy, which draws on these key areas, is needed to define the way in which the service will ultimately work.

Policies

Definition of policies is an important part of the planning process. Farmer (1995) states that 'policies are meant to spell out how your service puts its philosophy and goals into everyday practice . . .' by emphasizing that philosophies 'reflect broad purpose, values and beliefs and . . . might be seen as the ideal to aim towards.' Farmer continues 'a policy must be realised and . . . must be able to be put into practice.'

Policies should take into account not only the aims and goals of the individual service but should also consider the overall place of the service in the strategic direction of the organisation in which it is based.

Operational policy

An operational policy is the basis for all further development of specific policies and procedures. The operational policy directs the overall view of what the service may contain, how the service may be utilized, the number and type of staff required and the level of input from other departments. It specifies the aims and objectives of the service and underpins the details of everyday functioning in a clear and unambiguous way. The policy should include a description of all the major functions of the service. It should also clearly state the nature of relationships with other departments and service providers, and the responsibilities of the service to the patient.

In addition to the operational policy, specific policies concerning, for example, patient medications or access to inpatient beds, may need to be developed and established early in the planning process. Some policies that apply in other areas of the Trust or hospital, eg. manual handling and occupational health and safety, might be adopted as they stand. All policies should be integral to the development of the day care service and need to be reviewed regularly and added to as warranted.

The aims of an operational policy for a palliative care day centre might be:

- To provide day care facilities for a defined group of patients.

- To facilitate symptom control for patients without the necessity of admission to an inpatient bed.

- To provide an integrated approach to caring for patients in the community involving family doctors, primary health care teams and social services.
- To provide activities for patients whilst providing respite for carers.
- To enhance the physical functioning of the patient through input by allied health professionals.
- To provide assessment of needs for a defined group of patients.
- To provide emotional and spiritual support to those attending the service.
- To provide physical care, such as bathing and wound care, to those attending the service.
- To provide a forum for group work and patient education programmes.

The objectives of a policy should cover the details of how each of these aims can be met. This would include consideration of the referral mechanism, staffing levels, staff composition and responsibilities, access to inpatient and pharmacy services, alongside a description of the ideal premises and arrangements for transport. Furthermore, systems need to be in place to ensure communication with other services, and for the collection of data. These components of a policy are described in detail below.

Referral mechanisms

Family doctors, community palliative care teams, primary care teams and inpatient units form the basis for sources of referral to palliative day care services. Often day care services are provided as part of a larger palliative care service and it may be the first point of referral for some patients. A referral form should be developed that provides sufficient information to enable staff to decide whether to offer a place within a day care service, or whether input from the community palliative care team or admission as an inpatient would be more appropriate.

Staffing levels

The mix of skills and disciplines of the day care staff team will depend on the availability of both funding and suitably qualified staff. Many services provide a level of nursing and medical staff but are unable to provide allied health input. Allied services can however, greatly enhance a patient's experience of palliative day care. Examples are included in subsequent chapters. Where a half or full time equivalent post is not possible, then employment on a sessional basis should be considered. Volunteers may sometimes be able to provide particular specialist services.

Staff composition and responsibilities

Many palliative day care centres have a doctor who provides care on a sessional basis each day. A 'clinic' style arrangement may be most suitable for services where the doctor is available to see patients at particular times. The doctor may be someone who is already working within the wider palliative care service, or may be a family doctor who has an interest, skills and education in palliative care.

The levels of nursing staff should be set according to the number of patients expected to attend the day centre. There are no guidelines currently agreed regarding staffing levels for a day care centre. However, a number of services consider 10–12 patients to be the maximum level that one Registered Nurse and one other health care professional, such as an Enrolled Nurse or a Health Care Support Worker, can care for and assist. Consideration should be given to the need to cover these staff whilst on leave, be it planned annual leave or sick leave. Nursing staff responsibilities vary depending on the needs of the local patient population and the philosophy of care provided, but can include the following:

- the day to day organisation of the service and management of staff providing care;
- accepting patient referrals and assisting in the review of patient suitability in conjunction with the other members of the multidisciplinary team;
- management of the caseload;
- assessment and supervision of patient care, including coordinating the multidisciplinary care plan;
- performing appropriate nursing procedures such as wound dressing, administering blood transfusions or other intravenous therapies offered by the service;
- ensuring relevant and timely records are kept for each patient;
- organising transport for patients to and from the centre;
- ensuring close liaison and communication with all services involved in the patient's care;
- providing an environment in which psychosocial care can be provided.

The role of the nurse in providing a therapeutic environment is discussed further in Chapter 5. The importance of this environment cannot be underestimated. An ethnographic investigation within a palliative day care unit illustrated that the provision of a social environment for patients where they are able to express themselves through light-hearted talk was possibly as important as the provision of one to one counselling by a staff member (Langley-Evans and Payne 1997).

Allied services have an important role. The skills of a physiotherapist and occupational therapist can enable patients to maintain optimum functionality for as long as possible, and can assist the planning of care at home when a patient begins to deteriorate. The assistance of a social worker can be invaluable in providing not just emotional support but also practical advice on how to plan for the financial aspects of care.

The services of a diversional therapist can be invaluable. A diversional therapist can develop individual activity programs and has the ability to offer a wide range of activities to patients, thereby allowing the interests of patients to be identified and met. Other therapists that would enhance the formulation of these activity programs are music therapists and art therapists; these therapists provide an important avenue for patients to express themselves and are described in more detail in Chapter 6. The services of a hairdresser several times each week allows the patients to care for their appearance. This can enhance feelings of well being and improve body image.

The services of volunteers can add greatly to a day care service. Volunteers can be specifically recruited to support aspects of care that the service may wish to provide such as card players or assistance with outings. Often advertisements in the local paper or in newsletters of local interest groups may generate applications. As well as being company for the patients, suitably trained and supervised volunteers can often provide some of the 'value added' services, such as massage or other complementary therapies.

Formal education sessions should be provided to volunteers following interview and acceptance onto a volunteer programme. The following is an example of some of the objectives set for participants to meet by the end of the volunteer education sessions (D Griffiths, personal communication):

- an understanding of the principles of palliative care;
- to be aware of the psychosocial needs of the dying, their relatives and friends;
- knowledge of procedures to report to staff if any issues or concerns arise;
- awareness of the necessity of confidentiality;
- awareness of one's own attitudes to death and dying;
- awareness of infection control;

- knowledge of cultural and spiritual aspects of care;
- awareness of communication strategies that will enhance the caring role;
- awareness of caring for oneself when undertaking volunteer work.

A handbook containing guidelines can be a useful reference tool for volunteers. The handbook should describe the aims and objectives of volunteer support, what the volunteer does and does not do, as well as how the volunteer may access personal supervision and support. Volunteers should receive ongoing formal support and feedback within an appropriate framework to maintain the standard of the service. It is important to ensure that volunteers are not seen as a substitute for nursing or allied health staff; their function should be to support the care given by core staff, not to replace paid staff.

Communication with other services

It is vital that any changes in the care and condition of a patient are communicated to all the parties involved in caring for that patient. The family doctor should be informed about any recommendations regarding medications or care, if possible by fax on the same day. Other services such as district nursing, social services and not least the patient's carers should be informed of any relevant changes or problems identified. Good lines of communication also ensure that referrals continue to flow.

Access to inpatient beds and pharmacy services

The process for admission to an inpatient bed, when necessary, either on the same site or in the nearest hospice, should be a feature of the policy. The person in charge of the day care centre at that time would be responsible for providing information to the patient's family doctor regarding any changes in care.

Generally day care services do not provide an outpatient pharmacy service; patients could be provided with prescriptions to be dispensed at a pharmacy outside the hospital setting as necessary. It should be clarified during the planning of a day care centre who will take responsibility for patient medications and prescriptions. Although most patients will bring medications from home and most prescriptions will continue to be written by the patient's family doctor, there will be instances when a patient may require a prescription as a result of care provided by the day care service. An evaluation of possible costs and a service agreement with a pharmacy to provide an outpatient service (and to track costs), should be established.

Premises

Ideally, the day care centre should offer spacious and comfortable facilities, including:

- ◆ A main sitting area where patients can socialise with one another. Facilities for those wishing to watch television or to smoke need to be considered.
- ◆ An assisted bath in a bathroom with sufficient space for the nurses to assist the patient from either side.
- ◆ Office space for the nursing staff and medical staff to hold records, complete documentation and to meet.
- ◆ A consulting room for the medical staff, preferably containing at least one bed in case a patient needs to rest, or for other therapies to be undertaken.
- ◆ A room that may also be used for music or art therapy, counselling or complementary therapies, or interviews.
- ◆ A gym space. This can be very useful for rehabilitation or assessment of mobility, even if it is an area that may be simply screened off from the main sitting area.
- ◆ A room specifically fitted for hairdressing, if this service is being offered.
- ◆ Direct access to the outside. A garden area or sitting space can be important as some patients may wish to garden or simply rest outside.

Transport arrangements

Transport can often be a thorny problem for palliative day care services. If transport is unavailable, or its cost is prohibitive the service may be unable to deliver care to all the patients that require it. Care should be taken when establishing the budget for a day care service that transport costs are included.

In some instances, if resources are available, the buying of a suitable vehicle and employing a driver or drivers is the best option. Taxi cards and contracts with taxi services may provide the required level of service to a day care centre that is just starting, although contracts need to be carefully monitored in terms of quality and reliability of the service provided. Some services use volunteer drivers. However, the provision of vehicles and insurance issues need to be properly investigated and addressed to ensure patient safety.

Collection of data

For routine documentation

The decision as to whether case notes should be kept separately for day care patients or held as part of the community record is a local one. However, it is important that the notes are updated by all members of the multidisciplinary team contributing to care and that the notes follow the patient, so that if the patient is admitted the record of care is accessible.

There should be regular team meetings where planned individual programmes are recorded and progress noted in the case record. Review of these records can provide some reflection of the progress or deterioration of a patient over time. Following the initial assessment after admission to the service, a review period should be negotiated with the patient and clearly documented. There are instances when patients have been admitted to palliative day care and have subsequently improved on both a functional and emotional level to the extent where palliative day care is no longer the most appropriate form of care for them. In order to assist the patient in identifying ongoing needs or establishing improvements, setting a definite review period allows the patient and the health care professionals to monitor independence and respond appropriately to changing patient needs.

For audit and evaluation

In order to demonstrate the successful establishment of the service an annual quality improvement programme should be implemented. The collection of information that would be helpful in ensuring ongoing support for the service could include:

- establishing the number of patients using the service and the types of care required;
- demonstrating satisfaction of the patients and carers with the service through the use of routine questionnaires;
- determining the effect of offering day care on the workload of the community palliative care team and patterns of usage of inpatient beds;
- documenting the uptake of voluntary services offered;
- calculating the daily cost of care.

This topic is covered in greater detail in Chapter 7.

For the minimum data set

The development of a minimum data set for collection of information regarding the activity, demographics and coverage of palliative care services remains in its infancy in some countries. A national census of palliative care services was undertaken in Australia in 1997 and 1998 collecting patient activity data and a summary of patient related activities (State of the Nation Report 1998). In total, 14 palliative day care services reported operation across Australia. In Australia each State or Territory determines what information it requires and from which aspects of service delivery, be it home based care, inpatient or day care services. It has been suggested that this provides a basis for the wide variety in the structure of palliative care services across Australia particularly in relation to inpatient and community palliative care (Jellie and Shaw 1999).

In recent years the implementation of the Australian National Sub-Acute and Non-Acute Patient Classification (AN-SNAP) has been underway. This funding classification system was developed for rehabilitation; psychogeriatric evaluation and management; maintenance care and palliative care patients. Within these groups of patients a number of classes were identified. For palliative care patients 33 classes were identified, 11 for overnight patients and 22 for ambulatory patients, (Jellie and Shaw 1999).

For ambulatory palliative care patients, the information that should be collected for AN-SNAP is as follows:

- Phase of care (stable, unstable, deteriorating, terminal care or bereaved).
- Resource Utilization Groups Activities of daily living (RUG-ADL), (a basic dependency scoring system).
- The age of the patient.
- Whether the patient is receiving medical care only.
- Whether bereavement care only is being provided.
- Whether the patient is receiving therapies only.
- Whether only nursing care or multidisciplinary care is being provided.
- A symptom severity score measured by the Severity Score Index developed by Palliative Care Australia (Jellie and Shaw 1999).

The full implementation of this system of data collection is yet to occur. Ultimately there will be cost weightings attached to the patient classification and this may guide funding formulas in the future. In the UK, the National Council for Hospice and Specialist Palliative Care Services (NCHSPCS) in collaboration with the Hospice Information Service at St Christopher's Hospice have led the development of a minimum dataset that covers broadly similar issues. Following a pilot scheme, routine data collection began in 1997. Individual reports are fed back to services and summary data made available as reports.

Marketing

Although awareness of the development of the service may have been raised during the needs assessment and data collection process, marketing and assisting local health care providers with identifying suitable candidates for referral must be undertaken. The target population for marketing constitutes potential referrers to the service. These should have been described earlier in the planning process, and include family doctors, local service providers and community health centres. However, it can also be important to promote the service to the community at large. Marketing literature can be produced, taking into account different requirements for patients, health care professionals and carers when preparing such information. The literature should provide referrers with details of the criteria and process for referral, exclusion criteria and any other specific conditions laid down by the service. Literature for patients and carers should be written clearly so that they can understand what the service can provide. Relevant issues that should be taken into consideration when producing patient and carer brochures are:

♦ what would happen if the patient became more unwell during their time at day care;

♦ the review process;

♦ how the patient's care will be communicated to other services that may be involved.

Strategies

The strategies that may be utilised in marketing include:

♦ An official launch. If there is a patron for the service or a local celebrity who may be willing to assist then media coverage may be greater. Invitations to a coffee morning or afternoon tea to all stakeholders, relatives of patients who may access the service and other interested parties can create the initial interest.

♦ Use of local media. Apart from local radio and television stations there are a number of specific newsletters prepared for target audiences such as family doctors or local acute hospital services. Articles placed in these publications can raise awareness of the opening and provide a level of information regarding the model of service delivery.

- Holding an open day once each month, linked to an education pro-gramme or special lecture. This may be focused on patients and carers or on health professionals, and can ensure that the profile of the service remains high.
- Personal visits by staff to local referrers can help in assuring commu-nication and that questions or queries can be clarified.

Problems to avoid

A number of problems experienced by other centres to date can be avoided by careful planning during the development phase of a day care service.

Patient review and discharge policy

One issue that appears to be problematic for a number of services is the criteria for patient review. Experience has shown that some patients may stabilize following treatment or during their care by a palliative care ser-vice. In some cases, the patient may have a much better prognosis than originally thought. Criteria for review, reassessing needs and discharge should therefore be included in the criteria for care. The issue of caring for patients with diagnoses other than cancer, some of whom may have a longer period of terminal illness, is discussed in the final chapter. In the Thames Region palliative day care study 29% of patients in the centres surveyed had been attending for one year or more (Higginson *et al.* 2000). In addition, the mean time the longest-attenders in each centre had been attending day care was 4.5 years (range 1–12 years). There may be instances when an aged care group may possibly provide a different outlook and meet the needs of the person more appropriately.

By establishing review and discharge criteria in advance, and encour-aging participation by all members of the team, a policy and procedure can be constituted that is 'owned' by all the staff. This ensures that decsion-making on a one-off, ad hoc basis is avoided, and that the process will be viewed as fair and equitable by all concerned.

Funding and resources

In developing the proposal for a new day care service it is important that all aspects of funding, not simply revenue, are included. A capital replace-ment program must be considered from the beginning with a plan for maintenance and replacement of equipment over time. A smaller scale budget allowance should be made for funding a stock of provisions of supplements and small food items for immediate patient use. There are also times when special occasions arise, such as a patient's birthday, and minimal funding can provide for these small but important extras.

Staffing issues

Administrative support

Whilst those involved in the day to day delivery of a service are often anxious to ensure that patients have access to appropriate care, time must be set aside for development of lines of communication, documentation of the service (in addition to patient documentation) and day to day administration tasks. If there is the capacity to provide some administrative assistance then this is ideal, but the Registered Nurse still needs to identify opportunities to continue to develop links and alliances with other services. Sometimes the pressure of delivering the care can leave little opportunity for such activities. It is wise to plan from the inception of the service a certain amount of time to pursue networking activities to ensure the continued development and maintenance of the service.

Leave cover

If the day care centre is part of a wider palliative care service then provision could be made for a staff member from another part of the service to cover planned leave. Sudden absences such as those for sick leave are harder to plan for, but if the service has provision for a casual bank of staff then often a Registered Nurse who is experienced in the area can provide relief. Ideally there would be an allocated person, who is familiar with the day care service, to provide continuity and cover.

Conclusion

Setting up a day care service can offer opportunities to look at developing new and innovative ways to deliver care. To start a service from scratch is a rare opportunity to reflect on current practice and future directions. The challenge for a new service exists in ensuring that it does not duplicate existing resources, and provides an appropriate setting for patients to have their needs assessed on an ongoing basis. Patients may value the social aspects of day care as a means of allowing them companionship and access to activities that may otherwise be unavailable. Equally the healthcare professionals may value the opportunity to monitor a patient's progress in a setting where appropriate resources are available without admitting the patient and separating them from their home life.

In establishing a new day care service, there are issues and problems that will arise over time that may be different from those faced by older or long-established services, but there will also be triumphs and enlightening moments. Staff could consider recording the course of their service planning and opening. Documenting and publishing these experiences will ensure that others can learn from the process.

Summary points

- When considering establishing a day care service ensure all relevant local service providers are consulted and informed.
- Develop unambiguous criteria for admission, review and discharge.
- The development of an operational policy will enable the identification and inclusion of all appropriate support services from the outset.
- Develop a quality improvement plan during the inception of the service to guide evaluation and data collection.
- When marketing the service plan for ongoing events to maintain the profile of the service in the local community and service providers.

References

Farmer, S. (1995). *Policy development in early childhood services.* Newtown, Sydney, Community Child Care Cooperative Ltd.

Higginson, I. J., Hearn, J., Myers, K. and Naysmith, A. (2000). Palliative day care: what do services do? *Palliative Medicine,* 14, 277–86.

Jackson, A. C. and Donovan, F. (1999). *Managing to survive managerial practice in not-for-profit organisations.* Sydney, Allen & Unwin.

Jellie, C. and Shaw, J. (1999). *Palliative care information development. Progress report on the minimum data set for palliative care.* Canberra, Australian Institute of Health and Welfare.

Langley-Evans, A. and Payne, S. (1997). Light-hearted death talk in a palliative day care context. *Journal of Advanced Nursing,* 26, 1091–7.

Neale, B., Clark, D. and Heather, P. (1993). *Purchasing palliative care: A review of the policy and research literature.* Occasional Paper 11, Trent Palliative Care Centre, Sheffield.

Robbins, M. (1993). A framework for assessing palliative cere need. In *Needs assessment for hospice and specialist palliative care services: from philosophy to contracts.* (ed. M. Robbins), p5. Occasional Paper 4. National Council for Hospice and Specialist Palliative Care Services, London.

State of the Nation. (1998). *Report of National Census of Palliative Care Services.* Palliative Care Australia Inc., Canberra.

Wiles, R., Payne, S. and Jarrett, N. (1999). Improving palliative care services: a pragmatic model for evaluating services and unmet need. *Palliative Medicine* 13, 131–7.

5

Psychosocial day care

Cynthia Kennett

Every aspect of life is affected when an individual faces terminal illness. Fear of death, of symptoms, of treatment, anxiety about relationships, ability to cope or manage finances can all contribute to making the world a very unfamiliar and unsafe place. A psychosocial model of day care can facilitate an environment in which it feels safe to address many of these problems. St Christopher's Hospice Day Care Centre opened in 1990 and adopts a psychosocial approach to care.

The meaning of the term 'psychosocial' in the context of palliative care has been the subject of much debate (Field 2000). For the purposes of this chapter, psychosocial day care is used to describe a model of care in which patients spend a day at a hospice with a minimum of clinical interventions; this will be described in detail below. Before patients attend St Christopher's Day Care Centre, their physical symptoms should have been controlled so that attention can be directed to psychological and social needs. In addition, this approach offers spiritual care, and it will be shown that it can be a means of fostering hope in those who attend.

Provision of a psychosocial model of palliative day care requires the facilitation of an environment in which individuals can access their own resources. The American psychologist Carl Rogers developed client-centred therapy on the conviction that each individual has sufficient innate resources to deal effectively with whatever traumas, conflicts, or dilemmas he or she might experience. He maintained that the task of the helping professional was to facilitate an environment for growth by attending to three core conditions; (1) empathy, (2) unconditional positive regard and (3) congruence (Rogers 1951). The task of day care centre staff working within a psychosocial model is to create an environment in which people with advanced deteriorating disease can continue to find meaning and purpose in life.

Modern treatments for cancer have resulted in patients living longer with their disease; palliative medicine improves the control of physical symptoms, but even though patients may be comparatively well physically, it is not uncommon for their emotional and social life to be in ruins. Such patients can be described as experiencing social death (Sweeting and Gilhooly 1991). It is for these people that a psychosocial approach to day care has been developed. For palliative care to be effective 'Control of pain, of other symptoms and of psychological, social and spiritual problems is paramount. The goal of palliative care is the achievement of the best possible quality of life for patients and their families'. (WHO 1996). That is to say, physical and emotional care must go hand in hand.

The American psychologist Maslow proposed a hierarchy of needs which, he believed, were responsible for human motivation, drive and initiative (Maslow 1968). This hierarchy provides a useful tool for illustrating how total care can be offered (Fig. 5.1). It demonstrates the absolute necessity for distressing physical symptoms and social concerns to be addressed in order that an individual can transcend the circumstances of daily life with terminal illness and find meaning and purpose, or to use Maslow's word, to actualise.

This can present a daunting challenge to health care professionals. What does it mean in practice? Perhaps the key is to remember that

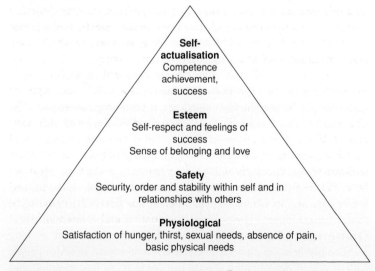

Fig. 5.1 The hierarchy of needs as identified by Maslow (1968).

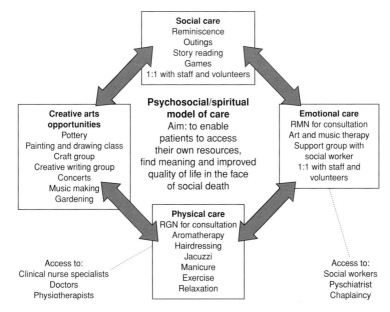

Fig. 5.2 St. Christopher's Day Centre.

'interventions' are not the answer to every problem. In 1996 Saunders wrote: '. . . the longing for significance and meaning goes beyond our own capacity to fulfil but we can try to create an atmosphere in which others find a freedom to make their uniquely personal journey.'

Figure 2 shows in diagrammatic form how a multiprofessional team can work together to provide an environment which facilitates improved quality of life. This is the focus of the work in the day care centre at St. Christopher's Hospice. The rest of this chapter should be read with reference to Figs 1 and 2 as the various aspects of the work are presented within the context of the theories of personal growth and development outlined above. It also illustrates that there are no clear demarcations between attention to the needs of the body, mind and spirit; they are inextricably linked: 'The whole approach has been based on the understanding that a person is an individual entity, a physical and a spiritual being.' (Saunders 1996).

Attention to physiological needs

The role of the day centre nurse

Patients with terminal illnesses are probably faced with greater physical needs than at any other time in their life. Much time is spent receiving medical interventions, having distressing symptoms controlled and monitored. Because physiological needs can become all consuming, other needs may be neglected and it is as if the patient remains stuck at the bottom of Maslow's hierarchy. Clearly, for an individual to be able to move up the hierarchy towards improved quality of life physical problems have to be resolved satisfactorily. However, this is not primarily the task of the staff of a day centre operating a psychosocial model of care.

For patients attending this day care centre it is the St. Christopher's Nurses at Home, liaising with oncologists and palliative medicine specialists, GPs and community services who provide the on-going symptom control. However, this is linked with the nursing care that is available in the day care centre. Day care centre nurses need to be able to use their skills flexibly and creatively in order to provide the support and safety necessary for patients to be confident enough to turn their attention away from their disease. They have to be quick to respond to new symptoms, to act as a resource if patients have anxieties about medication or wish to discuss treatments, and to liaise appropriately with other members of the wider team which includes the doctors, physiotherapist and dietician. They also provide a certain amount of hands-on physical care, bathing and feeding patients if this is required.

Day care centre nurses are not only concerned with the physiological needs of the patients; they play a vital role contributing to the safe and stimulating environment that enables patients to access their own resources. The nursing care is not an end in itself and the successful day care centre nurse has a broad, mature view of the role, a thorough understanding of individual quality of life issues and an interest in collaborating with professionals from other disciplines in their work with day care patients.

Attention to physical needs can lead to a greater sense of safety, security, order and stability within self and in relationship with others

Complementary therapies

When patients have experienced so much that has felt invasive and harsh, complementary therapies help to restore pleasurable feelings about the body, Sonia told the aromatherapist: 'It is nice to be touched without being investigated and told something is wrong'. Complementary therapies have a role to play in both physical and emotional care. They are hands-on interventions which work in conjunction with conventional treatments and aim to promote relaxation and induce feelings of well-being that can help to cope with the stress of illness. Therapists report that comments such as: 'It's the only thing that has made me feel human again' are a frequent response to therapy. There is a wealth of literature relating to the use of these treatments in palliative care and technicalities will not be described here (Wilkinson 1995, Pearson 1998).

At St. Christopher's, aromatherapy, reflexology and massage are offered. These are the complementary therapies most frequently offered in palliative care units but the range and scope of the service varies in each centre. St. Christopher's day centre patients may be referred by any member of the team or may refer themselves. It is also possible for an individual to choose to attend for a complementary therapy appointment without linking in with a whole day in the centre. Although no specific claims are made about control of physical symptoms patients frequently report that they have been affected. Brian said 'I feel very relaxed and soothed, my pain has eased', and patients who have been treated with reflexology often spontaneously report improved bowel function. The relationship with the therapist can enable patients to use the safety it affords to share deeply felt problems and confidences; 'It has given me space to think about things'.

Attention to personal appearance—hairdressing, manicure and dress

It is not unusual for patients to be reluctant to venture out of their homes because of their altered appearance and accompanying changes of body image. Hair loss, and how to deal with it, can be a cause of great distress, as can be the problem of excessive weight loss or gain which may be the result of the disease or treatment. A general lack of energy can result in a downward spiral of diminishing self-esteem and motivation for self-care.

A sensitive hairdresser can advise and support patients in a variety of ways. For those suffering hair loss, discussions around whether to have the head shaved, whether to wear a wig and how it should be styled can give the patient back some choice and control. An understanding of the impact of hair loss and encouragement to try new styles as the hair regrows can contribute significantly to restoration of self-esteem and confidence. It is interesting to note that some patients will insist on having a perm or another long and tiring procedure when they are clearly extremely unwell, and in some cases within days of death. This appears to be an indication of how important appearance is to some people's sense of self. On one occasion when a very sick lady had returned to the ward after a perm her daughter came to thank the hairdresser for 'the very caring perm' her mother had received.

Similarly a manicure or the offer of a shopping trip for new clothes, with a wheelchair if necessary and transport on hand, can also facilitate a patient's restoration of self-esteem. After prolonged reliance on others rediscovery of personal choice and purchasing power can provide a vital step towards improved quality of life.

Some specific interventions which facilitate emotional safety

The role of a psychiatric nurse in a day care centre

A day centre nurse with a qualification in psychiatric nursing offers the opportunity of addressing symptoms of mental disturbance in an unthreatening way. By making available one to one support for patients who may be experiencing panic attacks or suicidal thoughts they can be helped to understand their symptoms and find new ways of coping with them. It may be that such patients have been referred to a psychiatrist, in which case the day centre nurse would work closely with him or her. However, many people who are terminally ill experience anxiety and depression without a diagnosis of mental illness (McDonald *et al.* 1999). This can be understood as a normal reaction to the circumstances in which they find themselves, and by having someone available to address these problems considerable relief is obtained.

One woman, Kate, who had been having regular sessions with the psychiatric nurse because of daily panic attacks had experienced a marked improvement and said, 'To know such calmness and peace, even if just for a short time, has been wonderful, something I cannot remember feeling for a very long time.'

Art therapy and music therapy

Words are not always the most easy or useful way to communicate painful or frightening feelings. Art and music therapy provide other ways in which patients can access their own coping resources. Linda was surprised after her first art therapy session and said 'I looked at what I had drawn and saw it was myself. It showed how I was feeling. I'm really looking forward to next week.'

Therapists work to establish a therapeutic relationship with the patient within a safe and confidential environment. This can enable an individual to reflect on the use of the art materials, or music making, and how it links with their personal life experiences. The focus of the work is on the process of art or music making, not on making a product. (Pratt and Wood 1998, Aldridge 1999). Art and music therapies may be offered on an individual basis or take place in a group in which participants find support from each other by sharing experiences, as well as from the therapist.

Art and music therapists are not offering instruction in technique. Patients, staff and volunteers often need to have the distinction between a therapy group and class explained. Both have their part to play in providing a range of therapeutic creative opportunities, but it is not correct to describe all arts-based activities as art therapy.

Discussion support group

Some patients with a terminal illness can experience intense loneliness when it seems that everyone around them is carrying on with their normal lives. 'To meet with someone else in the same situation' is a wish often expressed by people who are referred to St. Christopher's day care centre. In common with the experience of Langley-Evans and Payne (1997) staff notice that much informal discussion and comparison of experiences takes place during the day. It has also been found that a more structured discussion group can be useful. This was requested by a younger group of patients that attends this day centre on a Thursday. It is each individual's personal choice whether to join the group or not. Some go regularly and it is the focus of their day, others attend intermittently according to how they are feeling. It is facilitated by a social worker who is experienced in group work, in a room away from the day centre and is confidential. The discussion is patient led and may on some occasions be about deeply emotional problems and on others light hearted and seemingly superficial. It is never insignificant. One young woman who attended the group summed it up by saying 'When I am here I am myself, when I am at home I am a person with cancer'. On reflection that is a remarkable statement.

Some patients report a feeling that there is a perception of stigma attached to being linked with a hospice. George, a day care centre patient was talking about his family and friends and said '. . . they don't understand, they think that once you're in a hospice it's a dead end, you're finished. That's what I thought originally. Someone needs to educate them'. Patients report that talking together in the day care centre can sometimes help them to find ways to communicate better with 'the outside world'.

Support from the social work, welfare department and chaplaincy

Some patients attending day care may have lost their role in society and means of support, resulting in anxiety about coping. In order that they are able to feel safe and confident they frequently need help with practical and financial problems. Liaison with community support services can provide personal and social care at home. In addition there is ready access to the hospice social work and welfare departments at St. Christopher's that offer counselling for emotional problems and assistance with the complexities of benefits. Similarly, for patients for whom religious faith is, or has been, important the chaplaincy can provide an additional source of strength. About once a month the chaplain also joins day centre staff for a non-religious 'remembering friends' time. This informal gathering of patients who choose to join in is an opportunity to acknowledge the losses experienced when day centre acquaintances die.

Nurturing self-esteem and fulfilment

For a few patients attending the day care centre the experience of the atmosphere in the company of others, including staff and volunteers, can be sufficient for their needs. For people who are new to the day care centre or who are particularly low in energy it is important that they are not pressured into any social interaction or activity they would prefer to avoid. Michael, a new patient who had spent part of his first day in the smoking room away from the day care centre said 'I didn't think I was going to enjoy coming, I was afraid we'd all be sat round and made to join in, it wasn't like that at all. I'll come back next week'. It is of paramount importance when patients are first introduced to the day care centre that they are informed of the opportunities on offer and clearly understand that they have choices about what they can do.

The role of creative arts

Everything that has been described so far contributes to facilitating a safe environment for personal growth, and space in which patients can be creative. Recognition of the value of the Arts in healthcare is not new although there is little literature describing evaluated projects. There are, however, examples from ancient Greece, through medieval times to the present day, which illustrate the benefits to health of an environment that embraces the arts (Kaye and Blee, 1997). In 1973 Peter Senior organised a multi-disciplinary arts team to work in health centres and hospitals in three health districts in Manchester. This was the start of Hospital Arts Manchester, which has since developed into Arts for Health, an internationally recognised organisation (Senior, 1998). In 1985 The Attenborough Report on the Arts and the Disabled made a significant contribution to raising awareness of the need for change. It included the following statement about health care: . . . The arts are frequently seen as an optional extra—in the social services as something to be added when resources allow, and in hospitals as a 'comfort' rather than an integral part of the healing and caring process. Arrangements which are far more comprehensive and systematic are needed. (Attenborough 1985).

The particular value of the arts in a hospice setting was embraced in a philosophy statement produced by the Board of Directors of Connecticut Hospice in 1976: 'Hospice affirms life and focuses on quality of life. To this end, hospice embraces and views the arts as an important and essential component of care. Hospice believes that the arts can enhance the personal living and working environments of patients, families and caregivers.' (Bailey, et al. 1990). The provision of 'systematic and comprehensive arrangements' has been recognised at St. Christopher's as essential if the patients are to be able to access their creativity.

A range of creative arts is offered by a team of paid professional artists with teaching qualifications who interact with the individuals in their groups as students rather than patients. The tutors work very closely with the rest of the team of staff and volunteers so that the physical needs of the participants are met and do not impede the creative process.

It is the philosophy of the centre to pay as much attention to the quality of the provision of these opportunities as is paid to any medical treatment. We look for highly qualified tutors and patients report how much they appreciate their expertise and the quality materials provided for their work. Many patients joining the groups are new to the experience and come with mixed feelings. To lessen anxiety it is important that the group is efficiently planned and organised so that new participants are introduced and helped to start as soon as they feel ready, whilst those who are already established can continue their work from week to week. At St. Christopher's we have found it particularly helpful to have two or three skilled volunteer helpers working with the tutor to provide sufficient one to one attention.

When patients are engaged in a creative activity they are not disturbed by consultations or medical procedures unless they themselves report symptoms requiring immediate attention. Casual interruptions by well meaning visitors admiring the work are not permitted without the expressed wish of the individual artist.

There is a different creative or social activity organised each day and a file containing photographs and information is available for nurses referring patients. They discuss the variety available in order that each individual may choose to attend on a day that seems interesting to them. It can be difficult to make a choice, in which case one day will be suggested with the option of changing to another. A brief description of the arts activities in the day care centre follows, with comments from patients and facilitators. It is recognised that other palliative day care centres offer different programmes, and stimulating the exchange of ideas between hospices is an important part of the managers' role.

Pottery

Clay is a unique material, very therapeutic to handle and great fun to play with. Patients are invited to join the group to make a variety of objects according to their choice. The facilitator is highly qualified in ceramics and able to teach sculpting, modelling and specific pottery techniques such as coiling, slabbing, use of moulds, slips and glazes. St. Christopher's is equipped with a kiln so that the process can be completed on site with minimal risk of damage to the work.

There is a relaxed atmosphere of concentrated energy in the pottery room. Sometimes there is very little conversation as potters are absorbed in their individual work; at other times there is convivial social interaction with individuals providing mutual support and exchanging ideas among themselves. It is very rare for anyone who has become involved in the pottery group to leave for any reason other than deteriorating health. It is apparent that the stimulus provides food for thought and conversation during the week, and potters come back next time with new ambitions for their next piece. Frequently, a model or piece of pottery will be made as a gift. Patients have expressed deep satisfaction from being in a position to give something to friends and relatives when they have had to

Fig. 5.3 A patient absorbed in pottery.

receive so much as a result of their illness. It seems that it can be a way of redressing the power imbalance. Many people who have received the work have told us how much they value having something tangible with which to remember a relative or friend.

Art workshop

The art workshop offers an opportunity to learn new skills in painting or drawing or to rediscover existing ones. The skilled facilitator is able to work with a group of artists who have differing abilities. Some people have not drawn or painted since school days when they may have been convinced that they were no good at art, while others have won awards in national competitions or sold work in the day care centre annual exhibitions.

There is a wide range of materials on offer, including watercolour, pastels, acrylics and charcoal. Occasionally there have been requests for oils but the turpentine fumes have caused feelings of nausea so this medium is not now included in the available materials.

The workshop is held in the Garden Pavilion, a newly acquired freestanding building in the garden of St. Christopher's where the members of the group particularly appreciate the feeling of being in a 'studio' right away from hospital or hospice connections.

Fig. 5.4 A patient enjoying his creativity.

Fig. 5.5 Discussing ideas while painting a mural.

There have been exciting new challenges offered to the group by the outreach education organised by the local Dulwich Picture Gallery. Guest tutors from there have brought reproductions from the gallery and run workshops in portraiture, charcoal, pen and wash, collage and egg tempera using the Great Masters for inspiration. The willingness to take risks and 'have a go' in these workshops has been truly remarkable and the partnership with the Gallery has strengthened community links.

The value of the creative process in leading to self-discovery should never be underestimated. The case study in Box 5.1 illustrates how engaging in the arts helped one woman to transcend the circumstances of her illness.

Box 5.1 Case study—art class

Jane, a woman in her late fifties who had to retire early from her health professional role came to the day care centre with many misgivings. Because of her background she had a strong aversion to talking with other people about their diseases and described herself as a recluse. However, she was severely limited by her breathlessness and bored, anxious and depressed at home. At the hospice Jane often needed to be by herself, did not enjoy eating with the other patients and chose to go home early. Her strength was her courage to continue trying; she wanted to rediscover her painting and drawing skills. When she was convinced that there were no set rules of how to use the day centre she agreed to go straight to the art room when she arrived, using an electric wheelchair to maximise independence. If she wished, she sat alone. No one was in the least offended if she left the room or went home early, we only asked to be told where she was. With sensitive encouragement and constructive criticism Jane's work has gone from strength to strength. She often uses the workshop as a resource and then does most of her work at home. She has survived two winters and is now happy to mingle with other patients offering support when they discuss their symptoms and treatments. She has found new self-esteem, enormous pleasure, admiration from friends, family and strangers, and a new way to talk to her family. She also describes a change in how she feels about her approaching death, being able to face it with a measure of calm she had not thought possible.

Fig. 5.6 a and b Communication can be facilitated by sharing arts activities.

Crafts

There is a wide range of crafts which are easily accessible to people who are terminally ill. Some of the ones that have been most enthusiastically received have been mosaic work, enameling, sugarcraft and sweet making, various projects with dried and pressed flowers, decoupage and painting on silk, ceramics and glass. Most of the projects are accomplished in one to three sessions and care has to be given in choosing crafts that can be completed in a realistic time scale. By having more than one craft available patients are able to choose a short or slightly longer project. At St. Christopher's the craft group has also worked on collective large-scale ventures, which have proved very popular.

The example in Box 5.2 shows how a patient found unexpected strengths to address his complicated problems in his own way. The intervention provided by the facilitator was to show John a new skill, the rest he did himself.

Box 5.2 Case study—crafts

John, a former lorry driver, had had an oesophagectomy. He had considerable pain and communicated by writing which he found very frustrating. He spent several hours in the day care centre decorating a cake with painstaking care in exquisite sugarcraft for his eleven year old son to give to his mother, John's estranged wife, for her birthday. He had never done anything like it before and felt an enormous sense of achievement. He reported that while he was concentrating on the decoration he was unaware of his pain.

Creative writing

Patients attend the creative writing group at St. Christopher's for a variety of reasons and continue to attend because the group fulfils their needs: the need for companionship, for self-expression, the need to boost self-esteem and to gain a sense of purpose. For some the group becomes profoundly important. One patient who had difficulty waking and dressing stayed fully dressed all night, so determined was he to come to write the following morning.

To be effective the group needs to offer an opportunity to explore thoughts, feelings, memories, ideas and imagination in a private, safe, supportive and non-censorious environment. Writing may take any form according to individual choice. Creative writing is frequently a struggle which is encouraged and valued as an important part of the process through which patients may express and explore feelings and fears. It can be a medium for growth and self-discovery. Bill said, 'I have discovered a dimension of myself that I never knew existed.'

Carefully selected and designed material in the form of the written word, a piece of music or art, an object or curio can provide external stimuli which can be important for group members who have not written before. Material must be accessible to all members as St. Christopher's serves a richly diverse community comprising many cultures and traditions. Examples of apparently simple materials that have been used in the group are a fan, a box, sea shells, passages from Alice in Wonderland and from Gulliver's Travels, and classical music.

Music and music making

At St. Christopher's there are regular short concerts given by a variety of artists, some professional, others local amateurs. Sensitivity to personal taste is important. In order that the majority get enjoyment from the programme, it seems that at least some of the items need to be familiar and the musicians need to be communicators as well as performers and engage with their audience. For some people the opportunity to join in and sing along is a source of great pleasure but not everyone is comfortable with this.

Gardening and horticulture

The gardening group is facilitated by an enthusiastic day care centre nurse with a keen interest and knowledge of gardening helped by volunteers, one of whom has considerable specialist knowledge. It has been received with tremendous enthusiasm by the patients who work at planting, propagating, sowing seeds and pruning while sitting comfortably at a table with their individual trays of equipment. The pleasure of handling the earth, seeing the plants grow and creating beautiful displays can have a profound effect on the wellbeing of the participants. There is the possibility of making gifts and contributing to fund raising, and although this is never required of patients they often appreciate feeling valued and independent if they are able to contribute by 'putting something back into the organisation'.

Reminiscence

Some patients do not wish to participate in arts and craft activities, but want to use their day in the centre for social interaction. The reminiscence group aims to meet the needs of some of these patients. Arigho (2000) writes of the value of this type of work when he says: 'Skilled reminiscence work helps to generate stimulating and enjoyable creative activities. It enables people to make new and rewarding social contacts, and it enriches personal and professional work satisfaction for a wide range of carers and other people who work with older clients.'

A large collection of materials facilitate reminiscence activities, ranging from war memorabilia to household utensils. The group usually has a theme as the focus for discussion and people from very different backgrounds engage in stimulating conversations. Participants are invited to choose the topics, which may also include games and quizzes.

Humour in the day care centre

The use of humour is valuable in promoting well being (Bain 1997, Dean 1997). Spontaneous laughter in a group may be far more effective than arranging some activity aimed to produce laughter. Sense of humour is very personal and a comedian can seem funny to one person but dull and patronising to another. Facilitating a relaxed environment in which laughter is common needs organisational skill to make the day flow smoothly with a minimum of fuss experienced by the patients.

Evidence for the value of psychosocial care

There is increasing pressure to demonstrate the value of the care given in palliative day care centres. There are very few evaluated studies of arts projects, but one such was carried out at St. Christopher's in 1997 when an exhibition of the patients' creative arts work was mounted as part of the day centre programme. There were three aims of the study:

(1) to gain insight into the creative experience of patients with advanced terminal illness;

(2) to develop a clearer understanding of how a facilitative environment for creativity may be developed;

(3) to develop day centre practice through attention to patients' experiences.

A phenomenological approach was chosen to study 10 patients and 11 tutors and assistant facilitators who participated in in-depth, semi-structured, audiotaped interviews. Some examples of comments from the interviews follow. One member of the writing group who had worked with a scribe said: 'When I had no use of my hands I wasn't able to write, I watched through traumatic experiences, in fact I was seriously traumatised. For three years I could not write, I wasn't myself, but when I joined the hospice the first time it was like a miracle, I was brought back, and there I was, valuable, I was back from this trauma, I was able to concentrate, I am myself.'

A patient who had been reluctant to come to the day care centre but who joined the craft group said: '... very therapeutic, because thinking to myself oh, ... I'm too ham fisted for this type of tiny work I found that I was able to cope, and always when I looked round there seemed to be somebody worse off than myself, and they were coping, being able to do it, so I thought if they can do it, I can do it. So then I got into the swing of it and the next thing I know I was doing all the big jobs ... tremendous.'

A patient, recently retired, who participated in painting a mural said: 'I have really enjoyed it, it's been something to come out for. I don't think I'd have got up if I hadn't had to come here ... It gives you a reason for living, really ... and of course it's permanent which makes it more important to the people who took part'

One of the tutors who had facilitated a textile group in which a patient with motor neurone disease had directed work by nods and smiles said: 'There was a person who actually physically couldn't do anything ... but she was included as though she was the most able-bodied person in the room.'

The contents of all the interviews were analysed to identify main themes. These were enjoyment, enthusiasm, excitement, pride, surprise, achievement, sense of purpose, incentive to work to a goal, and permanence. They were interpreted as expressions of self-esteem, autonomy, social integration and hope. Further investigation of the literature relating to these aspects of psychosocial care led to a correlation of the study with work by Herth in 1995. It was possible to conclude that the essence of the phenomenon studied was hope (Kennett 2000).

Discharge policy

The majority of patients deteriorate and die within a year of referral to the day care centre, although the energy they generate makes it hard to believe just how ill they are. A number, however, experience remission of their disease and for these patients continuing to attend palliative day care is not appropriate. If the patient's condition seems stable and the oncology report confirms that the cancer is not progressing, and if there is reason to believe that deterioration is not likely within the next six months, then a carefully planned discharge will take place. Although this is good news for the patient, she or he often finds it difficult to leave the day centre as the creative and social activities seem to transform people's lives. Every effort is made to introduce discharged patients to services outside the hospice and to encourage their own initiatives to live their lives to the full.

Summary points

♦ Psychosocial day care acknowledges that patients' physical, psychological, social and spiritual needs are inextricably linked.

♦ An understanding of Maslow's hierarchy of needs and Rogers' person-centred approach is the foundation for the psychosocial approach in palliative day care.

♦ The creation of a facilitative environment enables patients with advanced disease to access their own innate resources and transcend the circumstances of their illness to find self-esteem, meaning and purpose in life.

♦ It is suggested that the hope fostered by individuals accessing social and creative opportunities plays a significant contribution to wellbeing.

♦ This chapter describes the psychosocial model of day care operated at St. Christopher's Hospice.

Acknowledgements

Grateful thanks are extended to the day care centre team whose work helped produce this chapter; Jill Alkin, Rebecca Bennett, Adrian Butchers, Lynn Harmer, Elizabeth Hawkins, Lesley Webb. Also to Epoh Beech, Lynn Harmer and Sharon Wallace for their photographs.

References

Aldridge, D. (1999). *Music therapy in palliative care. New voices.* Jessica Kingsley, London.

Arigho, B. (2000). *Age exchange reminiscence centre leaflet.* Age Exchange, London.

Attenborough, D. (1985). *Arts and disabled people. The Attenborough Report.* Bedford Square Press, London.

Bailey, S. S., Bridgeman, M. M., Faulkner, D., Kitahata, C. M., Marks, E., Melendez B. B. *et al.* (1990). *Creativity and the close of life.* The Connecticut Hospice, Connecticut.

Bain, L. (1997). The place of humour in chronic or terminal illness. *Professional Nurse*, **12**, 713–5.

Dean, R. (1997). Humour and laughter in palliative care. *Journal of Palliative Care*, **13**, 34–9.

Field, D. (2000). *What do we mean by 'psychosocial'?* Briefing paper. National Council for Hospice and Palliative Care Services, London.

Herth, K. (1995). Engendering hope in the chronically and terminally ill: Nursing Interventions. *American Journal of Nursing and Palliative Care*, **12**, 217–21.

Kaye, C. and Blee, T. (ed.) (1997). *The arts in health care, a palette of possibilities.* Jessica Kingsley, London.

Kennett, C. (2000). Participation in a Creative Arts Project Can Foster Hope in a Hospice Day Centre. *Palliative Medicine* **14**, 419–425.

Langly-Evans, A. and Payne, S. (1997). Light-hearted death talk in a palliative day care context. *Journal of Advanced Nursing*, **27**, 1091–7.

McDonald, M. V., Passik, S. D., Dugan, W., Rosenfeld, B., Theobald, D. E. and Edgerton, S. (1999). Nurses' recognition of depression in their patients with cancer. *Oncology Nursing Forum*, **26**(3), 593–599.

Maslow, A. (1968). *Towards a psychology of being.* (2nd edn.) Van Nostrand, Toronto.

Pearson, J. (1998). Complementary therapies: making a difference in palliative care. *Complementary Therapies in Nursing and Midwifery*, **4**, 77–81.

Pratt, M. and Wood, M. (eds.) (1998). *Art therapy in palliative care. The creative response.* Routledge, London.

Rogers, C. R. (1951). Client-centered therapy. Houghton Mifflin Co., Boston.

Saunders, C. (1996). Into the valley of the shadow of death. *British Medical Journal*, **313**, 599–601.

Senior, P. (1998). *Arts for health information pack.* Manchester Metropolitan University.

Sweeting, H. N. and Gilhooly, M. (1991). Doctor am I dead? A review of social death in modern societies. *Omega*, **24**, 251–69.

Wilkinson, S. (1995). Aromatherapy and massage in palliative care. *International Journal of Palliative Nursing*, **1**, 21–30.

World Health Organisation. (1996). *Cancer Pain Relief.* WHO, Geneva.

6

The role of the doctor in day care

Adrian J. Tookman and
Karen S. Scharpen-von Heussen

Introduction

The provision of palliative day care has increased as palliative care services have become an integral component of health care services in the United Kingdom. Traditionally, palliative day care centres have tended to be nurse-led, and there has been no consistent remit for the doctor in this setting. The role of the doctor is variable (Copp *et al*. 1998; Higginson *et al*. 2000). This variability reflects a spectrum of models of care that exist in palliative day care centres. These models of care range from social, with the limited involvement of doctors, to medical, where doctors have a substantive role (Eve and Smith 1994). The underlying philosophy of the multi-disciplinary team, the needs of patients, the geography of the unit, the skills of the clinical personnel, the referral patterns of the local oncologists and the resources of the unit may all influence the model used.

Consequently, a spectrum of medical interventions is seen in palliative day care. These interventions range from simple procedures such as vene-puncture (Copp *et al*. 1998; Higginson *et al*. 2000) through to intravenous infusions of blood or bisphosphonates (Hargreaves and Watts 1998), aspiration and drainage of effusions or ascites (Copp *et al*. 1998) and, in our practice, nerve blocks under image intensification. The social model places emphasis on social support and a centre employing this model usually has a limited medical service. The medical model considers that active interventions enable good quality symptom control; in such a centre the doctor is a vital resource.

Table 6.1 Medical interventions in day care (adapted from Copp et al., 1998).

Intervention	Units offering service (%)
Assessment	52
Liaison with GP	44
Advice and support	22
Clinical interventions and tests	21
Prescribing	18
Symptom control	15
Monitoring	12
Consult and advise	6
Emergencies only	5
Consultant clinic	3

Copp *et al.* (1998) reviewed the spectrum of medical interventions offered in a random sample of 131 palliative day care centres across the United Kingdom. 24% of the centres surveyed operated without the availability of a doctor. The percentage of centres offering medical interventions is shown in Table 6.1.

Palliative day care is often seen as a bridge between the hospice or specialist palliative care inpatient service and the community. In this chapter we explore the role of the doctor in palliative day care and we demonstrate how a day centre can enhance and extend its ability to support the needs of patients in the community and become an essential component of the 'package of palliative care' (Department of Health 1995). We shall illustrate this using the example of our own Day Therapy Unit at the Edenhall Marie Curie Centre, North London, England.

Why have doctors in palliative day care?

To support patients as part of a multidisciplinary approach

An important role of the day unit is to support patients aiming to normalise their life (Neale 1992). This support allows the patient to focus on ways to improve their wellbeing and to achieve the confidence to regain a role in society (National Council for Hospice and Specialist Palliative Care Services 1995).

The doctor's role is to provide the medical view, to act as the provider of clinical information and to present possible management approaches within the context of the multidisciplinary team.

It could be argued that the presence of a doctor creates the potential to medicalise the environment, and that patients may feel that they must display persisting symptoms to continue to attend the unit. In this paradigm illness, not health, would have status. Nevertheless it has been shown that patients want to be able to access medical input in a palliative day care environment (Sharma et al. 1993).

To address complex symptom control needs

In modern health care, with multimodality, multiprofessional treatments, patients' needs are increasingly complex. The doctor in day care has an important role in the holistic assessment of the management and the needs of these complex patients.

Patients with cancer now have longer courses of potentially disabling treatment and they survive longer (Coleman et al. 1999), often with more complex physical and psychological problems. They appear to have a greater expectation that they will receive treatment for their cancer, and that treatment will continue until late into the natural history of their disease. Moreover, patients are being referred earlier and they more readily undertake and accept cancer treatments.

There is also increasing acknowledgement that specialist palliative care clinicians have an important role in addressing the needs of patients with non-malignant diseases—a group currently underrepresented in palliative day care (National Council for Hospice and Specialist Palliative Care Services 1998; Kite et al. 1999) These patients, too, have complex physical and psychological symptoms, but the natural history of these illnesses, and their prognoses, are often less predictable. These factors provide a challenge to clinicians in palliative day care units.

Edwards et al. (1997) demonstrated that only 10% of patients referred to a social day care centre were referred for a doctor's opinion or for symptom control. Despite this, initial assessment revealed a high prevalence of uncontrolled physical symptoms, poor correlation between patient problems and the reason for referral, and a lack of regular medical review; these cases required subsequent medical input.

To communicate with other professionals

The doctor has a role in communicating with primary care teams and specialists in the acute hospital and a role in interacting with both community and inpatient specialist palliative care services. Good working relationships with these services are essential for continuity of care. In addition, community patients often have the wider health care team reviewing their management. It is essential to maintain rapid and effective communication with these external agencies to provide high quality care.

Direct liaison between medical professionals can be helpful in facilitating further medical interventions or decision making in the community. Often no single team has the wide range of skills needed to address all components of patient care and sharing, rather than 'taking over', care can promote seamless care.

To provide a resource to the multidisciplinary team

The key to high quality symptom control is collaborative working (Abrahm 1998) and the importance of teamwork in palliative care is well recognised (Hull *et al.* 1989; West 1990). The professional interaction between doctor, nurse and other team members will often determine whether the team works effectively (Lowe and Herranen 1981). Good communication and respect for the skills of professional co-workers are believed to be the cornerstones of effective teamwork.

In practice, acting as a resource comprises two main elements. First, it entails providing clinical cover when a member of the multidisciplinary team is concerned that the patient needs a medical review. Second, it entails acting as a source of information, describing and explaining diagnoses, prognoses, the effects of treatment, implications of treatment or non-treatment and principles of treatments offered to patients. Members of the multidisciplinary team are then able to utilise the information for their own particular work with patients.

To ensure safe practice

The doctor has a responsibility to ensure safe practice. This is of particular importance when complementary therapies are offered. Patients have expectations when coming to a specialist clinical setting that any treatment offered is safe. If unmonitored therapies are adopted there are risks both to the patient and to the centre. The doctor's role is to assess effect, to monitor and to integrate therapies into the clinical setting. By monitoring the clinical aspects and response to the therapies the doctor can also ensure that the therapist is not exposed to patients with medical contraindications. This is particularly important for the risk management component of clinical governance.

Education

Palliative care services are generally accessed through primary care or hospital consultants (Gaffin *et al.* 1996). In some respects these professionals are the 'gatekeepers' to specialist palliative care and palliative day care services. Their perceptions of the value of day care will affect referral patterns. Education of these gatekeepers is critical in reinforcing the role and the overall value of day care for patients requiring palliative care. It can help to make referrers more aware of the skills possessed by the palliative day care team. Informally, education occurs on a day to day basis, as referrers observe the effectiveness of care delivered by the unit. Formally, educational programmes in palliative care should include the role and value of day care.

What skills does the doctor need?

All palliative care physicians should have expertise in communication, and should be able to provide high quality advice on symptom control both to patients and to other health care professionals. A strong grounding in general medicine and a good working knowledge of oncology is vital. However, in palliative day care medical consultation is enhanced by the acquisition of skills that are additional to those developed within an inpatient setting.

In day care, assessment and management planning occurs over minutes or hours rather than over days. A doctor must be able to make accurate, effective and rapid diagnoses, treatment decisions and management plans. This allows provision of information and advice that a patient can understand and act on. In addition, straightforward, understandable management plans, effectively communicated, will allow community health professionals to observe and monitor their patients.

Assessment

The initial consultation is a scene-setting event with the aim of enabling the patient to relax and to begin to understand the role of the palliative day care service.

It is essential, at this time, to obtain a detailed medical history, especially when assessing complex symptom control needs. This allows the patient to give a biographical account of how their illness has affected them and had an impact upon their life. It allows them to describe their own personal experience. The patient should be given time and permission to relate events or problems that they may have regarded as too trivial to discuss with other teams. They should be offered the opportunity to discuss concerns and to offload anxieties about diagnosis and previous treatments. It may be considered a luxury to spend a considerable amount of time taking a history but, in the context of a patient with an advanced illness, it is a necessity. The time afforded provides an opportunity to identify clues regarding patients' symptoms, about how they view their illness, their coping mechanisms, family dynamics, and their feelings about the future. These factors can be important in determining optimal treatment and intervention (Nolan 1998). It can be easy to make assumptions about patients' symptoms and for misdiagnoses and diagnostic uncertainties to be perpetuated. Thus, taking a detailed history will allow a clinician to confirm or challenge previous diagnoses.

When discussing assessment of patients it is important to stress the importance of 'pattern recognition'. This is a skill acquired by mature practitioners (Dreyfus and Dreyfus 1985), and is invaluable in a day care consultation. When taking a complete and accurate history and performing a clinical examination, the doctor can confirm a diagnosis if it fits into a recognised pattern. If the patients' symptoms do not fit this provides the opportunity for the diagnosis to be reviewed.

Management

In formulating a management plan, there are several important considerations. First, it is important to make any instructions explicit to avoid ambiguities, especially if changes involve titration of medication. Second, it is important to assess the patient's level of understanding of, and agreement with, the management plan in order to facilitate compliance. For the same reason, any regime implemented should be as uncomplicated as possible. Third, it is important to consider the patient's domestic situation, and the ease with which the community health professionals can monitor and complement the recommended management. Fourth, documentation is very important. All encounters with patients (appointments, telephone calls), any management plans, goals, follow-up and review dates should be recorded. Appropriate information from other sources should be requested so that sufficient details are available when the patient is seen. Although each of these considerations is valid when working with inpatients, in an outpatient consultation there is a restricted period within which such decisions can be made.

Employing the strategies above can improve organisational skills and facilitate high quality and high efficiency palliative day care.

Extending day care services—an example of the therapeutic model of care

We describe our unit as an example of a day centre where the doctor has a high profile (Box 6.1). The day therapy unit (DTU) reviewed its activities in 1997 and developed a therapeutic model of care to address the multiple and changing needs of our population of patients more effectively. This particular model places emphasis on a multidisciplinary approach. It offers medical, psychosocial and therapeutic care taking into account and reflecting the physical, emotional, social, spiritual, sexual and cultural needs of the patient and their significant others. One of the challenges was to construct a collaborative and co-ordinated 'package of care' that would use the broad range of skills offered by the professionals working in our unit (Box 6.2).

Box 6.1 Edenhall Marie Curie Centre day therapy unit

The day therapy unit (DTU) was developed in 1997 and officially opened in January 1998. The DTU has high profile medical involvement, with regular medical and nurse-led clinics. There is strong emphasis on collaboration with the multiprofessional team. Prior to 1998 a social day care existed, with less clinical input.

The DTU is situated in Belsize Park, North London, England. There is no official geographical catchment area, and patients are not denied access on this basis. However the main area served includes the boroughs of Camden and Islington, Haringey, Enfield and Barnet.

It is open for appointments (medical, nurse-led, physiotherapy, counselling, social work advice, complementary therapies) and social day care between 10:30 a.m. and 15:00 p.m. Monday to Friday. Counselling and physiotherapy appointments often run between 09:00 a.m. and 17:00 p.m.

There are over 200 patients registered at any one time.

Box 6.1 Edenhall Marie Curie centre day therapy unit *(continued)*

Philosophy of care of Edenhall day therapy unit

To provide an accessible specialist palliative care service to support patients at various stages of their illness. This service will complement the care offered by the local hospital trusts, primary care teams, oncology centres and local palliative care support teams. The aim is to maximise the patient's quality of life using a therapeutic approach in an informal setting, with the patient determining the meaning of their 'quality of life'.

Professionals from the multidisciplinary team plan and deliver care taking into account, and reflecting, the physical, social, emotional, spiritual, sexual and cultural needs of the patient and their significant others. This care is planned and delivered without discrimination. Confidentiality is respected at all times.

Box 6.2 The multi-professional team

The multi-professional team comprises a core team whose members are directly involved with the clinical care of the patient, as follows:

Specialist Nurse—co-ordinates all the activities in the unit.

Two Staff Nurses—monitor patients' progress and support them through their programmes.

Clinical Nurse Specialist—runs two outpatient nurse-led clinics per week undertaking assessment, care planning and evaluation of programmes.

Consultant—there are 7 medical outpatient clinics per week. An image intensifier is available to provide real time X-ray images for screening and injection techniques.

Staff Grade Doctor—acts as a medical resource for the unit.

Psychosocial Team—includes social workers, counsellor, and art therapist.

Physiotherapist—devises individualised gym programmes, runs two hydrotherapy sessions per week and is involved with lymphoedema management.

> **Box 6.2 The multi-professional team** *(continued)*
>
> **Occupational Therapist** - facilitates patients' independence and activities of daily living.
>
> Additional members of the multi-professional team include:
>
> **Volunteer Organiser**—co-ordinates all volunteer activities within the unit including volunteer therapists.
>
> **Aromatherapist**—employed 4 days a week with 2 volunteer therapists.
>
> **Chaplain**—available to all patients attending the unit for spiritual or religious support/guidance.
>
> **Reflexologists**—two trained volunteer therapists attend once per week.
>
> **Dietician**—access to a specialist palliative care dietician employed by local community healthcare trust.
>
> **Healer**—one trained volunteer therapist attends once per week.
>
> Source: Adapted from Hopkins and Tookman (2000)

Access to the day therapy unit

Patients are usually referred by their community palliative care team, primary care team, oncologist or from the inpatient unit. Some have been recommended by other patients accessing the unit; they are usually seeking a structured system of support and often have further information needs. The indications for referral were outlined by Hopkins and Tookman (2000) in a paper on rehabilitation in a specialist palliative care unit:

+ Pain and symptom control advice.
+ Introduction to hospice care and preparation for death.
+ Support for both physical and psychological problems following definitive cancer treatment. Many patients express feelings of abandonment and often perceive that support is only available during acute treatment. Some of these patients may have early disease but significant physical and/or psychosocial morbidity.
+ Management of long-term physical and psychological disabilities due to their cancer treatment and/or the disease itself.

- ◆ Management of far advanced non-cancer conditions exploiting expertise in pain management and use of opioids.

Patients are assessed, offered a care package and allocated a key worker. They are then reviewed at regular weekly multidisciplinary meetings. The role of the doctor is pivotal in this process; he or she sees all patients at, or shortly after, referral.

Oncology patients are the largest proportion of patients referred to our day therapy unit. It is particularly important to recognise that these patients may present with obvious advanced cancer but may not be at a stage in their cancer journey where they can acknowledge this. The term 'the cancer journey' has been used to describe the patient's passage through all aspects of their illness (Barley *et al.* 1999; Feber 1998). The phrase implies a beginning, a process and an end. The cancer patient has a story to tell; often this story has not been listened to adequately. It is especially important to be aware of this in the palliative day care setting where patients may present early, with many unresolved issues and with unrealistic expectations. In this setting, much can be learnt about the complexity of the illness and about where the patient is in their cancer journey. The value of allowing patients the space to give a biographic account early in their visit to a day care centre cannot be underestimated.

Impact on inpatient services

The shift in model of care from social to therapeutic, the subsequent growth of the service offered, the more prominent medical input and the changing nature of referral pattern now influences our inpatient unit significantly. Figures from an audit of admissions to the Edenhall palliative care inpatient unit reflected the changing impact of our day care service. We compared 100 consecutive sets of notes from each of the years 1991 and 1998 (Scharpen-von Heussen *et al.* 2000), i.e. before and after the adoption of the new therapeutic model of care. We analysed the percentage of admissions referred from the community, hospitals and our day therapy unit. Over the seven-year period, the percentage of admissions to the inpatient unit referred from the DTU increased three-fold (from 4% to 12%). More dramatically, the percentage of planned admissions to the inpatient unit referred from the DTU increased ten-fold (from 1% to 10%) over the same period.

The expanded medical service has allowed for an increasing number of referrals of patients with both malignant and non-malignant conditions who have complex symptom control requirements. It is easier to make pre-emptive plans for admission in this population of patients who undergo regular monitoring and observation, with the opportunity to liaise with community carers in the process.

We would therefore suggest that the therapeutic model, which values medical input, bridges the gap between the community and the inpatient unit more effectively than did the more social approach to palliative day care that previously existed.

Rehabilitation in palliative care—the role of the doctor

Rehabilitation is a process of readaptation and involves an active approach to patients with cancer and other advanced illnesses (Hockley 1993). The day therapy team can be pivotal in rehabilitating patients and, as mentioned previously, the doctor has a key role in assessing the complex symptom control needs in this group of patients.

The document 'A Framework for Cancer Care' (Calman Hine Report 1995) supported the concept of cancer rehabilitation. As observed elsewhere, it is somewhat surprising that rehabilitation does not feature more prominently in current cancer care provision. To facilitate individuals with a cancer diagnosis to reach their full potential a focus on their rehabilitation needs is required in adjunct to their treatment and palliative care needs (David 1995).

Wells (1990) identified three groups of patients who would benefit from cancer rehabilitation:

- Those with good life expectancy, in whom treatment has left no residual disfigurement or disability.

- Those with good life expectancy, but with physical or psychological disability or disfigurement caused by treatment.

- Those with poor life expectancy following treatment failure or relapse following initial remission.

Specialist palliative care has the skills to address many of the issues that these patients present to us. A day therapy unit can respond to these rehabilitation needs in selected patients.

Conclusion

The provision of palliative care services has increased markedly over the last thirteen years and is now an integral part of health care provision in the United Kingdom. As a consequence, palliative day care provision has also increased. The palliative day care centre should facilitate the movement of patients through different environments (home, hospital and hospice) and be considered as an important bridge between the inpatient unit and the community.

We have described the Edenhall Marie Curie Centre Day Therapy Unit as an illustration of a therapeutic model of day care that does not polarise the importance of social support from the value of medical input. It values the collaborative care of the multiprofessional team and it adds a further dimension—that of 'therapeutic' care—to encompass the necessary skills of the wide range of professionals working together. Within this model the doctor is regarded as a resource, with particular skills to offer the collaborative partnership.

These skills include an ability to observe and monitor the changing needs of patients over a period of time, and to be able to recognise patterns of illness. In addition, ongoing communication with primary care and referring agencies and specialists is necessary to maintain continuity of care. These factors are especially important in view of the changing nature of cancer care, i.e. referrals of patients with earlier stage disease, patients with more chronic courses of disease, and with increasing numbers of referrals of patients with non-malignant conditions.

Traditionally, day care has been seen as a low-key 'Cinderella' part of a specialist palliative care unit and, because of its historically passive approach has had a low status when compared with inpatient and community specialist palliative care services. Furthermore, national documents have suggested that there may be distinct differences between hospice and specialist palliative care units (National Council for Hospice and Specialist Palliative Care Services 1997, 1999), and that palliative day care embodies the passive approach that predominantly focuses on patients spiritual, social and psychological needs. For us, this is an uneasy concept. In our opinion, hospice and specialist palliative care coexist. High quality symptom control requires easy access to skilled medical care and this should apply to care in all settings. To suggest that hospice and specialist palliative care should be separated is a regressive step. That there is a diverse approach to the management of patients should be seen as advantageous to the speciality. Clearly, a culture of evaluation and research into different models of care needs encouragement. This will ultimately result in finding the most effective approach to palliative day care in the future.

Summary points

◆ At present, a spectrum of medical input and intervention exists in palliative day care.

◆ The degree of input is dependent on the day care service provided, the skills of the doctor available and the philosophy of the unit.

◆ The doctor should be regarded as a resource, whichever model of care is in place.

◆ Patients referred for palliative care have increasingly complex needs. In day care there is a role for doctors in the assessment and management of such patients.

◆ The 'therapeutic' model of care places value on the role of the doctor in the day care setting whilst putting the medical role into context within the multidisciplinary team.

◆ This model provides a role for the doctor in the rehabilitation of palliative care patients.

References

Abrahm, J. L. (1998). Promoting symptom control in palliative care. *Seminars in Oncology Nursing* 14, 95–109.

Barley, V., Tritter, J., Daniel, R., Baldwin, S., Cooke, H., Rimmer, P. *et al.* (1999) *Meeting the needs of people with cancer for support and self management.* A collaborative project between: Bristol Oncology Centre; Department of Sociology, University of Warwick; Bristol Cancer Help Centre (Unpublished) Cited by Hopkins, K. F. and Tookman, A. J., *International Journal of Palliative Nursing,* 6, 123–30.

Department of Health (1995). *A Policy Framework for Commissioning Cancer Services: A Report by the Expert Advisory Group on Cancer to the Chief Medical Officers of England and Wales* (Calman-Hine Report). Department of Health and Welsh Office, London.

Coleman, M. P., Babb, P., Damiecki, P., Grosclaude, P., Honjo, S., Jones, J. *et al.* (1999). *Cancer survival trends in England and Wales, 1971–1995: deprivation and NHS Region.* Studies in Medical and Population Subjects no. 61. Cancer Research Campaign. School of Hygiene and Tropical Medicine, London; Office for National Statistics and The Stationery Office, London.

Copp, G., Richardson, A., McDaid, P. and Marshall-Searson, D. A. (1998). A telephone survey of the provision of palliative day care services. *Palliative Medicine,* 12, 161–70.

David, J. (1995). Rehabilitation: adding quality to life. In *Cancer care: prevention, treatment and palliation*, (ed. J. David), pp. 351–75. Chapman and Hall, London.

Dreyfus, H. and Dreyfus, S. (1985). *Mind over machine: The power of human intuition and expertise in the era of the computer.* New York, Free Press. Cited by Benner, P. and Tanner, C. (1987). *American Journal of Nursing*, 87, 23–31.

Edwards, A., Livingstone, H. and Daley, A. (1997). Does hospice day care need doctors? *Palliative Care Today*, 6, 36–7.

Eve, A. and Smith, A. M. (1994). Palliative care services in Britain and Ireland—update 1991. *Palliative Medicine*, 8, 19–27.

Feber, T. (1998). Design and evaluation of a strategy to provide support and information for people with cancer of the larynx. *European Journal of Oncology Nursing*, 2, 106–14.

Gaffin, J., Hill, D. and Penso, D. (1996). Opening doors: improving access to hospice and specialist palliative care services by members of the black and ethnic minority communities. Commentary on palliative care. *British Journal of Cancer*, Supplement. 29: S51–3

Hargreaves, P. N. and Watts, S. (1998). Intravenous infusions in a hospice day care unit—an acceptable option? *Palliative Care Today*, 6, 50–1.

Higginson, I. J., Hearn J., Myers, K. and Naysmith, A. (2000). Palliative day care: what do services do? *Palliative Medicine*, 14, 277–86.

Hockley, J. (1993). Rehabilitation in palliative care—are we asking the impossible? *Palliative Medicine*, 7(suppl. 1), 9–15.

Hopkins, K. F. and Tookman, A. J. (2000). Rehabilitation and specialist palliative care. *International Journal of Palliative Nursing*, 6, 123–30.

Hull, R., Ellis, M. and Sargent, V. (1989). *Teamwork in palliative care.* Radcliffe Medical Press, Oxford.

Kite, S., Jones, K. and Tookman, A. (1999). Specialist palliative care and patients with noncancer diagnoses: the experience of a service. *Palliative Medicine*, 13, 477–84.

Lowe, J. I. and Herranen, M. (1981). Interdisciplinary team. In *Hospice Education Program for Nurses,* (ed. US Dept. of Health and Human Services), pp. 1047–8. Publication No. HRA 81–27. US Dept. of Health and Human Services, Washington.

National Council for Hospice and Specialist Palliative Care Services. (1995). *Specialist Palliative Care: A Statement of Definitions,* Occasional Paper 8. National Council for Hospice and Specialist Palliative Care Services, London.

National Council for Hospice and Specialist Palliative Care Services. (1997). *Dilemmas and Directions. The Future of Specialist Palliative Care.* Occasional Paper 11. National Council for Hospice and Specialist Palliative Care Services, London.

National Council for Hospice and Specialist Palliative Care Services and Scottish Partnership Agency for Palliative and Cancer Care. (1998). *Reaching out: Specialist palliative care for adults with non-malignant diseases.* Occasional Paper 14. National Council for Hospice and Specialist Palliative Care Services, London.

National Council for Hospice and Specialist Palliative Care Services. (1999). *Palliative Care 2000. Commissioning through partnership.* National Council for Hospice and Specialist Palliative Care Services, London.

Neale, B. (1992). *Palliative care in the community: the development of a rural hospice service in High Peak, North Derbyshire, 1988–1992.* Occasional paper no. 7. Trent Palliative Care Centre, Sheffield.

Nolan, M. R. (1998). Outcomes and effectiveness beyond a professional perspective. *Clinical Effectiveness in Nursing,* 2, 57–68.

Scharpen-von Heussen, K. S., Ali. S., Brogan, G. and Exton, L. (2000). *Audit of emergency versus planned and appropriate versus inappropriate admissions. A comparison of 100 consecutive admissions from each year 1991 and 1998* (unpublished). Edenhall Marie Curie Centre, London.

Sharma, K., Olivier, D., Blatchford, G., Higginbottom, P. and Khan, V. (1993). Medical care in hospice day care. *Journal of Palliative Care,* 9, 42–3.

Wells, R. J. (1990). Rehabilitation: Making the most of time. *Oncology Nursing Forum,* 17, 503–7.

West, T. (1993). *The interdisciplinary hospice team.* Presentation made at Seventh International Congress on Care of the Terminally ill. Montreal, 1990: September. Cited by Cummings, I., The Interdisciplinary Team, In *Oxford Textbook of Palliative Medicine* (ed. D. Doyle, G. W. C. Hank, N. MacDonald) Oxford University Press, Oxford.

PART C.   EVALUATING DAY CARE

7

Audit in palliative day care; what, why, when, how, where and who

Julie Hearn

In the 1980s the UK experienced an explosion of monitoring, evaluating and assessing activity and organisations found themselves subject to increasing scrutiny and accountability for performance (Power 2000). By the late 1990s the emphasis had changed to quality, performance, and excellence. Clinical audit is at the centre of the reinvention of clinical governance in the UK health care system, and the use of appropriate performance measures and standards is central to audit. Audit approaches and methods are now well advanced in palliative care, though less so in palliative day care where the policies and provision of care appear to differ more than in other palliative care settings. In addition, the evaluation of concepts such as social support, key to the more 'social' approach or model of day care (Eve *et al.* 1994), raise new challenges.

Audit aims to improve care for patients and families by assessing whether we are doing the right thing well (Higginson 1998). This chapter will provide an overview of the principles of audit in palliative day care, and provide guidance for implementing audit into routine practice.

What, where, why and who?

What is clinical audit?

Clinical audit is the systematic critical analysis of the quality of clinical care. Clinical audit grew out of separate medical and nursing audits and is most suited to areas where doctors, nurses and other staff work in teams, sharing decision making. In palliative care, where ideally patients' concerns are discussed by all staff, clinical audit is more appropriate than nursing or medical audit because it reflects the multiprofessional and holistic approach to care (Ford 1990).

Palliative care developed from a desire to improve the quality of care for patients with advancing disease and their families. In the face of scepticism or reluctance to support this new specialty, evaluations were carried out early in the history of modern palliative care provision, such as the comparison of hospice services to home and hospital care (Parkes 1979, 1985; Hinton 1979). Hence, palliative care specialists have often led the way in developing methods to examine the quality of care for patients with cancer, and have sought to influence those working in oncology and other professions (Higginson 1993a; Hodgson *et al.* 1997). Audit is important to purchasers of health care because it provides tangible evidence that the service is seeking the most effective use of existing clinical resources and wants to improve the quality of care. This is becoming increasingly relevant in an era of clinical governance and competition for health care contracts (Clarke *et al.* 1995).

The audit cycle

Effective audit is a cyclical activity that includes three key stages (Fig. 7.1).

In the first stage, standards for the delivery of care are agreed. As discussed later, this process should make use of existing guidelines, draw on the experience of other organisations, or be guided by a formal review of the literature. Practice is observed and compared to the standards in stage two. Success can be demonstrated at this stage, but so can failings

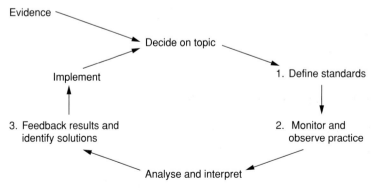

Fig. 7.1 The audit cycle

and the need for change. In the third stage, the results are fed back to those providing care so that new or modified standards can be set. The audit cycle is then carried out again (Shaw, 1980, 1989; Department of Health 1989, 1991). The cycle can be entered at any point. For example, it is possible to begin by implementing new standards and then conducting an audit to determine if these standards are being met.

Where should we focus our efforts?

Audit can assess the structure, that is the resources, e.g. number and qualifications of staff, the process e.g. discharge rate, or the outcome of care i.e. the change in the patient's quality of life or health status as a result of care (Donabedian 1980). The structural characteristics of care influence the process of care, and changes in the process of care, including variations in its quality, will influence the effect of care on health status and outcomes. Of these three approaches, outcome measurement most closely reflects what happens to patients and their families in palliative care because it can consider issues such as pain or symptom control, and aspects of quality of life. Box 7.1 provides some examples of audits carried out in palliative care, reflecting the range of topics that can be addressed in the various palliative care settings.

Box 7.1 Examples of published audits in palliative care

1. Auditing complementary therapies in palliative care: the experience of the day care massage service at Mount Edgcumbe Hospice (Byass 1999).

2. Opioid substitution to reduce adverse effects in cancer pain management—a prospective audit of clinical records (Ashby *et al.* 1999).

3. Death rattle: an audit of hycosine (scopolamine) use and review of management (Bennett 1996).

4. Problems of anti-coagulation within a palliative care setting: an audit of hospice patients taking warfarin (Johnson 1997).

5. Palliative care of cancer patients: audit of current hospital procedures (Sessa *et al.* 1998).

6. Assessment of GP management of symptoms of dying patients in an Australian community hospice by chart audit (Mitchell 1998).

Box 7.1 Examples of published audits in palliative care *(continued)*

7. Auditing palliative care in one general practice over eight years (Holden 1996).

8. Palliative care at home: an audit of cancer deaths in Grampian region (Millar *et al.* 1998).

9. Planning palliative care services (Finlay *et al.* 1992).

10. Patient preference for the place of death (Carroll 1998).

The research/audit interface

Research is a course of scientific study into a particular subject. It is not primarily concerned with comparing current practice to defined standards but is rather a more critical investigation of a subject in detail. Examples of research in day care include an investigation of patients' attitudes to the introduction of intravenous infusions in a day care service (Hargreaves and Watts 1998), and an exploration of the processes surrounding talk about cancer, death and illness amongst patients in one day care unit (Langley-Evans and Payne 1997). For a more detailed review of research in palliative care, and the associated problems and pitfalls, see Chapter 9.

The boundary between research and audit is not always distinct, and both processes can easily be used as an opportunity for high-quality education and training (Fig. 7.2). Audit is important for education and training because the structured review allows analysis, comparison, and evaluation

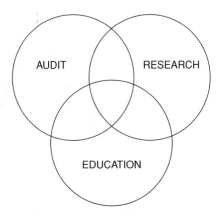

Fig. 7.2 The overlap between research, audit and education.

of individual performance, it promotes adherence to local clinical policies, and it offers an opportunity for publication of the results (Shaw 1993a). Evidence from research can feed into the very first stage of the audit process by helping to define the topic of an audit. Moreover, the advent of clinical governance has formalised the requirement for audit and the implementation of research findings into practice.

Why audit?

The tension between demands for care and the resources to provide it have increased the need for better information about clinical effectiveness in setting priorities (Fletcher *et al.* 1996, preface). Moreover, it has become clear that not all clinical care is effective and that outcomes of care are the best way of judging effectiveness. In the context of health and illness, outcome is usually defined in terms of the achievement or failure to achieve desired goals (Wilkin *et al.* 1992). Measuring outcome can therefore help to determine whether a particular treatment or particular intervention package is worthwhile (Bowling 1997).

In a literature review of day hospice care, Spencer and Daniels (1998) suggested it would be reasonable to assume that 'the aims, client groups and activities of each day hospice are congruent'. However, they highlighted that research has illustrated the variations in policies and priorities for practice in each day hospice result in each centre developing a specific identity and characteristics, and that day hospices do vary greatly in their structure and process. In healthcare in general, variations in care among clinicians and regions, not explained by patients' needs and not accompanied by similar difference in outcomes, have raised questions about which practices are best (Fletcher *et al.* 1996, preface). Hence, audit should serve not only to improve patient care but also to ensure resources are used effectively (Shaw 1993b).

Who: the costs and benefits of audit

Audit takes time and resources. These must not be underestimated and can include:

1. Time for all staff to prepare for the audit, to agree on the standards or topic, and to review the findings.
2. Time for some staff to carry out the audit, analyse the results, and document the findings and recommendations.
3. A commitment by all staff—managers, nurses, doctors, therapists and others—to consider the results and act upon the recommendations.

4. Resources to pay for the staff time involved, plus any other analytical or computing support needed.

As a result of the high costs of audit, it is important to ensure that the audit itself is as effective as possible or, put another way, what is the purpose of collecting data if the recommendations are not acted upon? The costs and benefits of carrying out clinical audit are summarised in Box 7.2.

Box 7.2 The costs and benefits of audit

The costs of not auditing care may include:

1. Extra inappropriate treatment or services, wasting the time and resources of patients and their families, and wasting staff time or resources which could be used elsewhere.

2. Admission to a hospice or hospital due to uncontrolled symptoms causing unnecessary suffering to the patients, the family and the staff.

Audit can help to improve care in the following ways:

1. Reviewing the quality of work and identifying ways to improve means that future patients and families will not suffer the same problems that occur at present.

2. Identifying areas where care is effective or ineffective allows better targeting of services.

3. Prospective audits with systematic assessments of patients and families during care can help to ensure that:
   – aspects of care are not overlooked
   – there is a holistic approach to care
   – new staff have a clear understanding of what areas to address.

4. Audit can help most palliative care patients and their families by focusing on routine practice rather than focusing on a few cases of special interest.

Defining outcomes in day care

The relevance or suitability of an outcome variable is defined by the purpose of care and by patients' expectations. The outcomes of disease have been described as the five Ds (Fletcher *et al.* 1996, p. 5):

(1) death: or survival from an illness;
(2) disease: a set of symptoms, physical signs, and laboratory abnormalities;
(3) discomfort: symptoms such as pain, nausea, and dry mouth;
(4) disability: impaired ability to go about usual activities at home, work, or recreation;
(5) dissatisfaction: emotional reaction to disease and its care, such as sadness or anger.

The influence of palliative care on survival time is marginal, and survival is uninformative about the patient's health before death (Rinck et al. 1997). Death and disability are therefore inappropriate health care outcomes in the measurement of palliative day care. However, the rationale for measuring quality of life in palliative care is clear: patients receiving an intervention should function and feel better than patients who do not (Porzsolt 1993). Measuring a patient's satisfaction with care is recognised as important in evaluating the discrepancy between their expectations and their experience (Lohr 1988). However, satisfaction is recognised as being a particularly difficult concept to measure, particularly when those providing care are often the same individuals as those conducting the audit.

Hence, there is a particular need to measure aspects of care that reflect the specific goals of palliative care, such as improving the quality of life before death, controlling symptoms and supporting the family (Higginson and McCarthy 1993).

Quality of life measures are often used to assess outcomes in palliative care. While early measures concentrated on physical function, newer measures include evaluation not only of the symptoms of the disease, but also emotional and psychological functioning. More recently aspects of social function and spiritual needs have been included. While the definition of quality of life is constantly debated, the areas or domains most frequently included are given in Box 7.3.

Tools for clinical audit in palliative day care

The purpose of measuring quality of life and the outcomes of patient care are summarised in Box 7.4.

In a recent literature review of outcomes measures in palliative care 12 potential clinical audit tools were identified and these are summarised in Box 7.5 (Hearn and Higginson 1997), along with the details of a recently developed palliative care outcome scale (Hearn and Higginson 1999). To determine whether a particular outcome measure would be relevant

Box 7.3 The domains of quality of life

- Physical concerns
- Functional ability
- Emotional well-being
- Psychological functioning
- Social functioning
- Occupational functioning
- Spirituality
- Sexuality
- Treatment satisfaction
- Financial concerns
- Future plans
- Family physical and emotional well-being

to an audit in a particular situation the following set of criteria, developed by Boyle and Torrance (1971), can be used:

1. Is it easy to apply?
2. Is it acceptable to responders?
3. Is it brief and inexpensive to administer?
4. Does it use precoded response categories?
5. Does it use an explicit time period of assessment?
6. Does it use unambiguous instructions for respondents?

Box 7.4 Reasons for measuring the patient's quality of life and the outcomes of care

1. To obtain more detailed information about the patient for clinical monitoring in order to aid and improve patient care.
2. To audit the care provided by determining whether standards are being met, and to identify potential areas for improvement.
3. To compare services, or to compare care before and after the introduction of a service, which can be of value in assessing the efficacy and cost effectiveness of a service.
4. To analyse the data generated using outcome measures and use this to inform purchasing bodies, thereby securing resources for future services.

Box 7.5 Measures for assessing the outcome of palliative care for people with advanced cancer (adapted from Hearn and Higginson 1997, with permission)

Name of measure	Number of items and domains covered	Setting developed in	Time to complete	Method of administration
An Initial Assessment of Suffering (MacAdam and Smith 1987)	43 (patient); mood, symptoms fears and family worries, knowledge and involvement, support	inpatient service	not known	patient completion or by professional interview
Edmonton Symptom Assessment Schedule—ESAS (Bruera et al. 1991)	9 (patient); pain, activity, nausea, depression, anxiety, drowsiness, appetite, well-being, shortness of breath	inpatient	few minutes	patient completion or with nurse assistance
European Organisation for Research on Treatment of Cancer—EORTC QLQ-C30 (Aaronson et al. 1993)	30 (patient); 9 multi-item scales including 5 functional, 3 symptom scales and a global quality of life scale (supportive care module under development)	outpatient	11–12 minutes	patient completion
Hebrew Rehabilitation Centre for Aged Quality of Life Index –HRCA-QL (Morris et al.' 1986)	5 (patient); mobility, daily living, health, attitude, support	community and hospice inpatient	1–2 minutes	professional completion
The McGill Quality of Life Questionnaire—MQOL (Cohen et al. 1995)	17 (patient); physical symptoms, psychological symptoms, outlook on life and meaningful existence	inpatient and outpatient	not known	patient completion
The McMaster Quality of Life Scale—MQLS (Sterkenberg and Woodward 1996)	32 (patient); physical symptoms, functional status, social functioning, emotional status, cognition, sleep and rest, energy and vitality, general life satisfaction, meaning of life	community, inpatient and outpatient	patients: 3–30 minutes; staff: under 3 minutes; families: approximately 3 minutes	patients, family or staff completion

Instrument	Description	Setting	Time	Completion
Palliative Care Assessment—PACA (Trent Hospice Audit Group, 1992)	12 (patient & relatives); symptom control, insight of patients and relatives, plans for placement	inpatient	few minutes	professional completion
Palliative Care Core Standards—PCCS (Ellershaw et al. 1995)	6 core standards and 56 process and outcome items (patient & carer); collaboration, symptom control, information, emotional support, bereavement support, specialist education for staff	inpatient	expected to take about 10 minutes	professional, patient, carer and the bereaved
Palliative Care Outcome Scale —POS (Hearn and Higginson 1999)	10 (patient & carer); pain, symptoms, anxiety, information, support, psychosocial items, wasted time, personal affairs	inpatient, outpatient and community	less than 10 minutes	patient or staff completion (2 versions)
Rotterdam Symptom Checklist—RSCL (de Haes et al. 1990)	34 (patient); physical and psychosocial symptoms	outpatient	8 minutes	patient completion
Support Team Assessment Schedule—STAS (Higginson 1993)	17 (patient & carer); pain and symptom control, psychosocial items, insight, family needs, planning affairs, communication, home services and support from other professionals	community and hospice inpatient	2 minutes	professional completion
Symptom Distress Scale—SDS (McCorkle and Young 1978)	13 (patient); nausea, mood, loss of appetite, insomnia, pain, mobility, fatigue, bowel pattern, concentration and appearance	inpatient	not known	patient completion in presence of an interviewer
The Schedule for the Evaluation of Individual Quality of Life—SEIQoL (O'Boyle et al. 1994)	5 domains nominated by the individual; 30 hypothetical scenarios are rated based on these domains and weights derived for each domain	community and inpatient	not known	patient completion as part of a structured interview

Staff could use these criteria to decide upon a measure to use, and thereby have an opportunity to critique each measure and make an informed choice as to which would be most relevant to their audit. None of the measures described in Box 7.5 were developed specifically to evaluate palliative day care, or tested fully in a day care service. Each of the measures described fulfils the Boyle and Torrance criteria to varying degrees, but none does so completely—it is questionable whether any such tool could be developed.

The systematic use of an outcome measure during audit can help ensure that staff perform a broad assessment of the patient and family. Such tools can be used to encourage staff to maintain a holistic approach to patients and families, evaluating all the quality of life domains and not simply symptom control. Each item of an established measure can be used in a training situation to encourage debate and review of practice across staff and professions. New staff may bring new experience or may need to be introduced to methods they have not previously used. The mechanisms for communication within an organisation, and access to services within the organisation and with local agencies, can also be discussed.

Staff need to be consistent in their rating of items on staff-completed outcomes measures, not only to ensure that meaningful audit data are collected, but also to facilitate communication between staff on different days and across professions. Case studies or fictional patients can be used to train staff to rate patients in a standard way. It is well known that the design and methodology of data collection can determine outcome (Nelson *et al.* 1998), therefore data collected for audit can only ever be as good as the method used to obtain it, and training is essential if an audit is to succeed.

When and how?

There is often antipathy towards audit by staff in general. In palliative care, this antipathy is based on arguments such as (Higginson *et al.* 1996):

1. There are no problems with our service because palliative care is high in quality and is self-auditing.
2. The outcomes of palliative care cannot be measured.
3. Resources, information and time are not available.
4. Audit looks at past practices, not at the problems that lie ahead.

Clinical audit requires the involvement of staff at all levels, and their cooperation is vital if the audit is to be successful (Ford 1990). Shaw (1989) described ten requirements for the successful management of audit: intention, leadership, participation, control, method, resources, guidelines, comparisons, conclusions, and feedback. Some key issues that need to be considered when trying to get staff involved in audit are the necessity to (Higginson and Webb, 1995, Higginson *et al.* 1996):

1 incorporate audit into routine practice;

2 share responsibility;

3 make time for audit.

When can we find time to conduct an audit?

Shaw asserts that clinical staff should be provided with the time, training and technical and clerical support required to conduct an agreed audit programme (Shaw 1993b). For audit to work organisational systems such as those outlined in Box 7.6 need to be established.

Box 7.6 Organisational commitments required to complete an audit programme

1. Training in audit methods should be available to all clinical staff.

2. Session time should be accounted for in staff contracts according to the frequency, duration and location of meetings, as well as for preparation and follow-up.

3. Technical and clerical assistance should be available for retrieving, tabulating and presenting the necessary data for an audit.

4. Management should make a commitment to ensure that the findings of the audit are acted on.

Training

Staff training can take place in two stages (Higginson and Hearn 2000):

1. A basic introduction to audit—objectives, benefits, tools.

2. A focus on advanced skills—motivation, data analysis and interpretation, feeding back results.

Basic training in audit should describe the objectives, benefits and difficulties of audit (Box 7.7). The barriers to audit described in this chapter should be explained, along with the suggestions of how to overcome them. Higginson (1993b) suggests the first stage of training in audit can be outlined using the mnemonic ASTRA: **Assess** current knowledge

Box 7.7 Objectives, benefits and difficulties in auditing palliative care (Hearn and Higginson 1997)

Objectives

1. Need to review a relatively new specialty that is expanding rapidly.
2. Personal goal of improving care.
3. External pressures to improve.
4. Practice varies throughout the country.

Benefits

1. The problems of patients and their families are considered in more detail.
2. Staff members are able to monitor the quality of their work and seek ways to improve it.
3. Audit provides a systematic way of thinking about the objectives and outcomes of care.
4. Identification of areas where care is effective and ineffective.

Difficulties in implementing change as a result of audit

1. There is inadequate communication of information from those present at the audit meeting to other staff members.
2. It is difficult to ensure that those with hands-on patient contact feel ownership of changes.
3. Difficulties may exist if the main communicator is resistant to change.

and attitudes; **Sell** the reasons for the audit; **Target** the training to areas of need; **Review** concerns and likely problems; **Agree** on an audit to be introduced and any further training required.

Staff at both ends of the managerial spectrum need to appreciate the concerns of others, and should be given the opportunity to question the purpose of any proposed audit in a non-judgmental atmosphere. Team meetings can be used to facilitate the implementation of audit using both a bottom-up and top-down approach; the responsibility for audit must be shared by the entire staff, throughout all grades and across all professions. Each member of a team will approach a topic from a different perspective, and the opinions of all should be given equal value, irrespective of who is taking the lead at any stage. Those unable to attend audit meetings could be updated by a colleague, or audit 'buddy', whom they have agreed to liaise with in order to keep informed (Higginson and Hearn 2000).

Specific time needs to be allocated to audit within the usual working hours of all staff involved, and sufficient coverage provided during this time to reassure the clinical staff that patient care is being maintained. Managers and staff need to agree on the time allocated for participation in audit and to find ways to incorporate this into the review of staff progress: participation in audit could be made explicit in staff contracts and the reasons for this discussed. In this way audit can become part of routine practice.

How can audit be established in day care?

The initial stages of audit are very important and often determine whether the audit is a success. Higginson (1993b) proposes another mnemonic, SPREE, to guide the setting up of an audit:

Small: when audit is introduced it should be inexpensive and simple, and cause minimum disruption to routine care. It is better to begin small and expand as audit becomes established.

Plan: there should be a clear audit plan and a commitment to it by all staff. This requires leadership from senior staff and the participation of all staff, plus a clear view of how the audit will evolve. There should be discussion among all staff about all the stages of the audit plan at the outset.

Regular: audit meetings, data collection, and the review of results must occur regularly, otherwise these may become lost in other aspects of care.

Exchange: it is helpful to exchange ideas within the audit group and with other groups locally to learn about each other's successes and mistakes.

Enjoy: this is an important aspect of audit. The intention of audit must be educational and relevant to clinical care. It is important that staff do not see audit as a threat, but instead feel that they own it. This attitude can be promoted if the staff feel that they have been involved in developing or choosing the methods.

Both staff dealing directly with patients, who will probably be responsible for collecting outcome data and implementing any recommended changes in practice, and those with less patient contact but with the power to implement changes, need to show that they are supportive of the objectives of the audit. Well planned audit meetings can help facilitate this process.

How can we ensure the success of audit?

For audit to be successful it is important to be able to measure successfully what we intend to audit. Some of the key issues to keep in mind are included in the mnemonic BRAVE (Higginson 1993b):

Borrow: use the standards, methods, and measures of others to save time and resources, if possible, and adapt these to local circumstances as necessary. Developing new measures and standards can be very time-consuming. It may lead to 're-inventing the wheel' and developing a standard or measure similar to one already published.

Reliable: reliable measures or criteria are needed if more than one person will assess the standards, otherwise time will be wasted and the results can be meaningless. Reliability is the stability and consistency of information provided by the measure, also sometimes referred to as the precision of the instrument. A measure is reliable to the extent that repeated measures under constant conditions will give the same result. Reliability can be enhanced by using the measure under controlled conditions, by ensuring that the assessors are adequately trained, by using unambiguous items, and by providing clear rating instructions (Bowling 1997).

Appropriate: appropriate standards and measures are needed so that the staff feel that the work in their setting is being assessed accurately.

Valid: measures and criteria that assess what the investigator sets out to measure are important if the audit is to be effective and to achieve the goal of improving the care of the patient and family. Validity has a number of components, and measures shown to be valid must also be reliable.

Easy: the methods must be simple enough to be understood and applied in routine practice. Ideally, information for an audit should be collected in monthly, weekly or daily practice.

Data analysis

The hypothesis being tested by the audit must remain the key focus of any analysis. The presentation of results as simple tables and graphs of numbers and percentages is often all that is required to demonstrate differences or similarities in the data collected during an audit. If more extensive analysis using statistical methods is required, this should be taken into account during the planning of the project to ensure that sufficient data are collected, for example, to detect a difference in results (if that is the required outcome). Simple guidelines for the presentation of data include:

- Use of tables to summarise large amounts of data.

- Graphs provide a good overview of results and can be used in place of tables in some instances, as long as the values are easily readable from the axes or supplementary data.

- 3-dimensional graphs can mislead the reader and should therefore be used sparingly.

When writing the final report it is useful to begin with an executive summary of the project, and a list of key recommendations that arise from the data. The full report should summarise the aims of the audit, include the methodology, describe the final results, and provide an interpretation of the findings, a discussion of the limitations of the data, and include suggestions of areas that should be considered for change.

Implementing results

Putting evidence into practice can be a lengthy, complicated process. A project evaluating the implementation of change on 17 areas of healthcare where there was a good evidence base highlighted that it can take years, not months, to change clinical behaviour (Wye and McClenahan 2000). The key lessons learned from that project were:

1. While getting high quality evidence takes a rigorous, and highly preplanned approach, successful implementation requires pragmatism and flexibility.

2. Start small and build incrementally.

3. Use what is already there, such as regular team meetings, educational events, communication forums, and build on previous work.

4. Target enthusiasts first.

Qualitative approaches to evaluation

Dying is a complex, dynamic process which changes with time. Qualitative approaches to research and evaluation, such as ethnographic studies, non participant observation, case studies, interviewing using open-ended questions, are all useful methods for obtaining data on a patient's subjective experience. However, patients participating in audit or research may feel under great pressure to provide socially desirable answers (Fakhoury et al. 1997) and a reluctance to criticise providers of care is well documented (Kelson 1995). The pressure to provide socially desirable answers may be intensified in face-to-face interviews, compared to self-administered questionnaires. Hence, whilst qualitative research can be used to elucidate specific issues or themes for future consideration and which could provide the topic for audit, using qualitative methodologies during an audit may result in information which has potentially limited generalisability to other patients.

Conclusion

Day care services have become an integral part of the provision of specialist palliative care. Patients are able to attend day care for a longer period than at an outpatient clinic or assessment, and there is an opportunity to make closer assessments of symptoms, to reduce isolation, to allow creative activity and to increase the patient's self-esteem and feelings of worth. Moreover, day care can establish an introduction to the inpatient hospice and its services, offer practical help, and provide respite for caregivers (Kaye 1992). Day care services can bring new therapies to patients, such as advanced symptom control, counselling, or complimentary therapies. These new therapies need to be evaluated and audited: otherwise hospices' resources and patients' time could be wasted.

Robust methodology is required to evaluate the experiences of patients in day care and their families and carers. Audit is the systematic critical analysis of the quality of clinical care, and is intended as an iterative process to help organisations to develop and improve practice. There are a variety of new and proven palliative care audit methods and measures that can be adopted into day care. Audit can be used to develop clinical protocols for treatment, or for the development of algorithms to predict patient problems and identify the need for other specialised care. In addition, clinical audit provides an opportunity for educating and training staff to work effectively and consistently.

Audit is perceived by most health professionals as beneficial to a service (Higginson *et al.* 1996), but finding the time for an audit can be difficult. Thomson and Barton (1994) suggest that this problem can be alleviated by incorporating audit into the daily routine.

Audit is here to stay and is now widely accepted, but it requires resources. Hence, it must be sure to benefit patients and families, be kept as simple and efficient as possible, and have a strong educational component. Further work is needed to evaluate the impact of different approaches and methods of providing day care so that we know which methods are most effective, and represent the most cost-effective use of resources.

Summary points

◆ Clinical audit is at the centre of clinical governance in the UK health system.

◆ It is the systematic critical analysis of the quality of clinical care.

◆ It can be used to provide tangible evidence that a service is seeking the most effective use of existing resources and wants to improve the quality of care provided.

◆ Audit takes time and resources and the costs of these need to be accounted for when planning an audit programme—clinical staff need to be provided with the time, training and technical and clerical support to conduct audit.

◆ Outcome measurement can evaluate what happens to patients and their families, and outcome measures can therefore be used to determine whether a particular intervention is worthwhile.

◆ It is important to use outcome measures that reflect the specific goals of palliative day care, including improving the quality of life before death, controlling symptoms and supporting the family.

◆ While no outcome measures have been developed specifically for use in palliative day care, there are a variety of new and proven methods and measures that can be adopted.

◆ It can take years not months to change clinical behaviour, therefore a clear plan for putting evidence into practice is required to implement the results of an audit.

References

Aaronson, N. K., Ahmedzai, S., Bergman, B., Bullinger, M., Cull, A., Duez, N. J, et al. (1993). The European Organisation for Research and Treatment of Cancer QLQ-C30: a quality-of-life instrument for use in international clinical trials in oncology. *Journal of the National Cancer Institute*, 85, 365–76.

Ashby, M. A., Martin, P. and Jackson, K. A. (1999). Opioid substitution to reduce adverse effects in cancer pain management. *Medical Journal of Australia*, 102, 68–71.

Bennett, M. I. (1996). Death rattle: an audit of hyoscine (scopolamine) use and review of management. *Journal of Pain and Symptom Management*, 12, 229–33.

Bowling, A. (1997). *Research methods in health*. Open University Press, Buckingham.

Boyle, M. H. and Torrance, G. W. (1971). Developing multiattribute health indexes. *Medical Care* 22, 1045–57.

Bruera, E., Kuehn, N., Miller, J. J., Selmset, P. and Macmillan, K. (1991). The Edmonton Symptom Assessment Schedule (ESAS): a simple method for the assessment of palliative care patients. *Journal of Palliative Care*, 7, 6–9.

Byass, R. (1999). Auditing complementary therapies in palliative care: the experience of the day-care massage service at Mount Edgcumbe Hospice. *Complementary Therapy in Nursing and Midwifery*, 5, 51–60.

Carroll, D. S. (1998). An audit of place of death of cancer patients in a semi-rural Scottish practice. *Palliative Medicine*, 12, 51–3.

Clark, D., Neale, B. and Heather, P. (1995). Contracting for palliative care. *Social Science in Medicine*, 10, 1193–202.

Cohen, S. R., Mount, B. M., Strobel, M. G. and Bui, F. (1995). The McGill Quality of Life Questionnaire: a measure of quality of life appropriate for people with advanced disease. A preliminary study of validity and acceptability. *Palliative Medicine*, 9, 207–19.

de Haes, J. C. J. M., van Knippenberg, F. C. E. and Neijet, J. P. (1990). Measuring psychological and physical distress in cancer patients: structure and application of the Rotterdam Symptom Checklist. *British Journal of Cancer*, 62, 1034–8.

Department of Health. (1989). *Working for patients. Medical audit: working paper 6*. HMSO, London.

Department of Health. (1991). *Medical audit in the hospital and community health services*. HC(91)2. Department of Health, London.

Donabedian, A. (1980). *Explorations in quality assessment and monitoring. volume 1: the definition of quality: approaches to its assessment*. Health Administration Press, Michigan.

Ellershaw, J. E., Peat, S. J. and Boys L. C. (1995). Assessing the effectiveness of a hospital palliative care team. *Palliative Medicine*, **9**, 145–52.

Eve, A. and Smith, A. M. (1994). Palliative care services in Britain and Ireland – update 1991. *Palliative Medicine*, **8**, 19–27.

Fakhoury, W. K. H., Mcarthy, M. and Addington-Hall, J. M. (1997). The effects of clinical characteristics of dying patients on informal caregivers' satisfaction with palliative care. *Palliative Medicine*, **11**, 107–15.

Finlay, I., Wilkinson, C. and Gibbs, C. (1992). Planning palliative care services. *Health Trends*, **24**, 139–41.

Fletcher, R. H., Fletcher, S. W. and Wagner, E. H. (ed.) (1996). *Clinical epidemiology: the essentials.* (3rd edn.) Williams and Wilkins, Baltimore.

Ford, G. (1990). Constructive audit. *Palliative Medicine*, **4**, 1–2.

Hargreaves, P. N. and Watts, S. (1998). Intravenous infusions in a hospice day care unit-an acceptable option? *Palliative Care Today*, **6**, 50–1.

Hearn, J. and Higginson, I. J. (1997). Outcome measures in palliative care for advanced cancer patients: a review. *Journal of Public Health Medicine*, **19**, 193–9.

Hearn, J. and Higginson, I. J. (1999). Development and validation of a core outcome measure for palliative care: the palliative care outcome scale. *Quality in Health Care*, **8**, 219–27.

Higginson, I. (1993a). Palliative care: a review of past changes and future trends. *Journal of Public Health Medicine*, **15**, 3–8.

Higginson, I. (1993b). Clinical audit; getting started, keeping going. In *Clinical audit in palliative care* (ed. I. Higginson). Radcliffe Medical Press, Oxford.

Higginson, I. (1993c) A community schedule. In *Clinical audit in palliative care* (ed. I. Higginson) pp. 34–7. Radcliffe Medical Press, Oxford.

Higginson, I. (1998) Clinical and organisational audit in palliative care. *Oxford textbook of palliative medicine*. (2nd edn.) (ed. D. Doyle, G. W. C. Hanks and N. Macdonald), pp. 67–81. Oxford University Press, Oxford.

Higginson, I. J. and Hearn, J. (2000). Palliative care audit: tools, objectives and models for training in assessment, monitoring and review. In *Topics in palliative care Vol. 4*, (ed. R. Portenoy and E. Bruera). Oxford University Press, New York.

Higginson, I. J. and McCarthy, M. (1993). Validity of the support team assessment schedule: do staffs' ratings reflect those made by patients or their families? *Palliative Medicine*, **7**, 219–28.

Higginson, I. and Webb, D. (1995). What do staff think about audit? *Journal of Palliative Care*, **11**, 17–19.

Higginson, I. J., Hearn, J. and Webb, D. (1996). Audit in palliative care: does practice change? *European Journal of Cancer Care*, **5**, 233–6.

Hinton, J. (1979). A comparison of places and policies for terminal care. *Lancet*, **1**, 29–32.

Hodgson, C. S., Hearn, J. and Higginson, I. J. (1997). The role of palliative care in cancer. *Oncology Today*, **16**, 7–10.

Holden, J. D. (1996). Auditing palliative care in one general practice over eight years. *Scandinavian Journal of Primary Health Care*, **14**, 136–41.

Johnson, M. N. (1997). Problems of anti-coagulation within a palliative care setting: an audit of hospice patients taking warfarin. *Palliative Medicine*, **11**, 306–12.

Kaye, P. (1992). *A to Z of hospice and palliative medicine*. p. 21. EPL Publication, Northampton.

Kelson, M. (1995). *Consumer involvement initiatives in clinical audit and outcomes*. College of Health, London.

Langley-Evans, A. and Payne, S. (1997). Light-hearted death talk in a palliative day care context. *Journal of Advanced Nursing*, **26**, 1091–7.

Lohr, K. N. (1988). Outcome measurement; concepts and questions. *Inquiry*, **25**, 37–50.

MacAdam, D. B. and Smith, M. (1987). An initial assessment of suffering in terminal illness. *Palliative Medicine*, **1**, 37–47.

McCorkle, R. and Young, K. (1978). Development of a symptom distress scale. *Cancer Nursing*, **101**, 373–8.

Millar, D. G., Carroll, D., Grimshaw, J. and Watt, B. (1998). Palliative care at home: an audit of cancer deaths in Grampian Region. *British Journal of General Practice*, **48**, 1299–302.

Mitchell, G. (1998) Assessment of GP management of symptoms of dying patients in an Australian community hospice by chart audit. *Family Practice*, **15**, 420–5.

Morris, J., Suissa, S., Sherwood, S. and Greer, D. (1986). Last days: a study of the quality of life of terminally ill cancer patients. *Journal of Chronic Diseases*, **39**, 47–62.

Nelson, E., Splaine, M., Batalden, P. B. and Plume, S. K. (1998). Building measurement and data collection. *Annals of Internal Medicine*, **128**, 460–6.

O'Boyle, C. A., McGee, H. and Joyce, C. R. B. (1994). Quality of life: assessing the individual. *Advances in Medical Sociology*, **5**, 159–80.

Parkes, C. M. (1979). Terminal care: evaluation of in-patient service at St Christopher's Hospice. Part I. Views of surviving spouse on effects of the service on the patient. *Postgraduate Medical Journal*, **55**, 517–22.

Parkes, C. M. (1985). Terminal care: home, hospital or hospice? *Lancet*, **1**, 155–7.

Porzsolt, F. (1993). Goals of palliative cancer therapy; scope of the problem. *Cancer Treatment Reviews*, **19(Suppl.A)**, 3–14.

Power, M. (2000). The evolution of the audit society, its politics of control and the advent of CHI. In *NICE, CHI and the NHS reforms*, (ed. A. Miles, J. R. Hampton and B. Hurwitz). Aesculapius Medical Press, London.

Rinck, G. C., van den Bos, G. A. M., Kleijnen, J., de Haes, H. J., Schade, E. and Veenhof, C. H. N. (1997) Methodologic issues in effectiveness research on palliative cancer care; a systematic review. *Journal of Clinical Oncology*, **15**, 1697–707.

Sessa, C., Pampallona, S., Carobbio, M., Neuenschwander, H. and Cavalli, F. (1998). Palliative care of cancer patients; audit of current hospital procedures. *Supplementary Care in Cancer* **6**, 266–72.

Shaw, C. D. (1980). Aspects of audit. 1. The background. *British Medical Journal*, **280**, 1256–8.

Shaw, C. D. (1989). *Medical audit. A hospital handbook.* King's Fund Centre, London.

Shaw, C. D. (1993a). Quality assurance in the United Kingdom. *Quality Assurance in Health Care*, **5**, 107–18.

Shaw, C. D. (1993b). Introduction to audit in palliative care. In *Clinical audit in palliative care*, (ed. I. Higginson). Radcliffe Medical Press, Oxford.

Spencer, D. J. and Daniels, L. D. (1998). Day hospice care-a review of the literature. *Palliative Medicine*, **12**, 219–29.

Sterkenburg, C. A. and Woodward, C. A. (1996). A reliability and validity study of the McMaster Quality of Life Scale (MQLS) for a palliative population. *Journal of Palliative Care*, **12**, 18–25.

Thomson, R. and Barton, A. G. (1994). Is audit running out of steam? *Quality in Health Care*, **3**, 225–9.

Trent Hospice Audit Group. (1992). *Palliative care core standards; a multi-disciplinary approach.* Trent Hospice Audit, c/o Nightingale Macmillan Continuing Care Unit, Derby.

Wilkin, D., Hallam, L. and Doggett, M. A. (1992). *Measures of need and outcome for primary health care.* p. 5. Oxford University Press, Oxford.

Wye, L. and McClenahan, J. (2000). *Getting better with evidence. Experiences of putting evidence into practice.* King's Fund, London.

8

The role of health economics

Hannah-Rose Douglas and
Charles Normand

Background

Health economics provides tools that are widely used in the evaluation
of health care interventions, and for setting priorities. While economic
evaluation in cancer therapies is widespread, there are few studies that
use economic approaches in the evaluation of palliative care (Salisbury
et al. 1999). There has been debate for almost twenty years about the role
of economics in the evaluation of hospice and palliative care (Bayer *et al.*
1983; Goddard 1989; Robbins 1998).

Evaluation in palliative care has always been difficult (Grande *et al.*
1996), not least because the services are provided for people near the end
of life, who often present with multiple and complex needs for care
(Billings 1998). Palliative care has developed as a mixture of public and
private provision, with extensive input from voluntary and charitable
organisations (Douglas *et al.* 2000). Provision has expanded rapidly,
ensuring that there is a service available in most parts of the UK,
alongside extensive developments of day care and home care teams. The
input of voluntary organisations has led to some diversity in the developments, and distinct philosophies of provision are visible (Spencer and
Daniels 1998).

Palliative care is, therefore, provided in a complex mixed economy
(Tierney and Sladden 1994). There is considerable interaction between
charitable organisations in the UK, such as Macmillan Cancer Relief and
Marie Curie Cancer Care, and statutory health and social provision. For
example, Macmillan Cancer Relief funds medical and nursing posts for a
fixed period within NHS hospitals and provides professional support for

some nurses employed by hospitals (Macmillan Cancer Relief Guidance for Finance Departments, private correspondence). District health authorities are now purchasing hospice care from the voluntary sector and developing fully funded NHS hospice services (Higginson *et al.* 2000b).

The reliance of palliative care on at least some voluntary fundraising has contributed to services being developed on a more ad hoc basis than other cancer-based services (Department of Health 1996). It may therefore be the case that the development has been driven more by the perceptions of the staff than by systematic evaluation (Torrens 1984; Payne 1996).

Palliative care services need to demonstrate their value to patients, their families and the general public (Goddard 1993). In the past, palliative care has avoided some of the financial and service development pressures that other sectors have faced. Its development has been largely at the local level, in a fairly autonomous environment, and with relatively little control by central government or the NHS (Department of Health 2000). As palliative care services have grown, and the volume of funds from government sources has increased, it has become clear that the government is taking an increasing interest in their funding and quality. This implies that they will be judged in similar ways to other services: 'By 2004, the NHS will invest an extra £50 million in hospices and specialist palliative care. The Department of Health will agree with the voluntary sector the core services that should be available, so that more patients will have access to these services, and the NHS will make a more realistic contribution to the costs of voluntary hospices. NHS and voluntary sector services will work more closely together' (National Cancer Plan 2000).

This leads to some dilemmas. Palliative care is perceived to be different from mainstream health services in important ways. For example, Abel (1986) suggests '[Palliative care services] break down the barriers of authority and status, bridge the gap between expert and non-expert, expand rights of the 'consumer' (and his/her family unit), increase acceptance of the course of nature.' Further development of palliative care, and indeed the maintenance of the current levels of services, is likely to be dependent on being able to demonstrate that they are cost-effective and can justify being given priority in the competition for public funds. Provision by voluntary organisations has potential advantages in terms of innovation and flexibility in service provision. At the same time, where providers are answerable to funders from different cultures (the NHS and the voluntary sector) this can make them more vulnerable.

It is clear that there is a need for palliative care to present its contributions in ways that allow comparison with other social and health services that compete for scarce resources. This is not straightforward, since there are reasons why it is difficult to apply some conventional evaluation tools to palliative care services (Normand 1996). This chapter considers some of these difficulties, and suggests ways in which economics can be applied more usefully to the evaluation of palliative day care.

How is palliative day care different from other health services?

Many of the ways in which palliative day care is different reflect degree. For example, it is more diverse than most other NHS-funded services. While people present with obvious, visible care needs, they also may attend day care because staff feel they live in situations of acute social isolation and where no other form of care is offered. There are high staff-to-patient ratios and the workforce is often dependent on voluntary as well as paid therapists and support staff. The effect of this on the provision of services is to not only make them more flexible and adaptable to individual patients' needs, but also to make them less stable and more reliant on the willingness of local people to support the service (Douglas *et al.* 2000).

The specific goals of palliative day care differ between patients referred to the service, and the outcomes of palliative care are less tangible than those associated with acute interventions. They are perhaps unique in considering quality of death alongside quality of life (Jarvis *et al.* 1996; Whynes 1997). It is difficult to identify and isolate particular services that contribute uniquely to goals associated with finding meaning and hope and that mean different things to different client groups (Spencer and Daniels 1998). Furthermore, palliative day care affects not only the patient but also family and carers, and does so in subtle ways. This presents serious challenges for the evaluation of these services (Box 8.1). Nevertheless it is important to overcome these difficulties.

Evaluation of palliative day care

Between 1997 and 2000 the Thames regions palliative day care study was carried out to evaluate the nature and effectiveness of palliative day care.

Box 8.1 Challenges to applying health care evaluation techniques to palliative day care

What makes a health care intervention relatively straightforward to evaluate?

Interventions that are relatively easy to evaluate have the following characteristics:

♦ They are highly structured, specific interventions, delivered in mostly the same way for all patients.

♦ They focus on improving physical health, with specific care pathways or algorithms to follow.

♦ The outcomes are clearly defined in terms of improvements in physical health (and length of life) and there are uncontested, accepted definitions of positive and adverse outcomes.

♦ The focus is on the patient alone and usually on a specific aspect of their health, rather than on social or pastoral needs, or the wellbeing of the whole family.

♦ The intervention (or service) is the accepted form of meeting a particular clinical need and is not substituting other similar services.

Applicability to palliative day care research

In nearly all these categories, palliative day care is different:

♦ It is not an acute intervention, and covers social as well as physical goals.

♦ It does not aim to provide the same pattern of care for all patients.

♦ It can be a relatively less intensive intervention, for example patients may only access a palliative care therapy once a week alongside more intensive active therapies.

♦ Different types of services are offered under the label of palliative care, reflecting differences in emphasis on various aspects of care. This dilutes any effects that might be observed for the service as a whole.

One of the aims of this study has been to explore ways of evaluating the costs and effectiveness of palliative day care services. Some of the early results have been published (Douglas *et al.* 2000; Higginson *et al.* 2000b).

The authors' experience of working on evaluation in palliative day care has confirmed an important point: it is vital to work closely with those experienced in service delivery. However, it has shown that economics can provide both some alternative ways of looking at services, and a framework for asking important questions. Some of these relate to the overall priority that should be given to palliative day care, how benefits derived from the service can be measured, what should be included in the range of services offered, and how best to ensure that the patients' needs are being met.

Some basic economics

The approach taken by economists always looks at two sides of a service— its costs and its consequences. Even services that bring great benefits may be poor value when costs are considered, and low cost services that do some good can be excellent value. The problem that always arises, but which is particularly difficult in this case, is how to assess the benefits, and how appropriately these are compared to the costs.

Measuring economic benefit for evaluation

The concept of 'benefit' in economics is different from the use of this term in the clinical world. In clinical trials, the change in a group of patients' health status is usually measured in an objective way by some improvement in their physical status. There are some underlying principles that govern this type of evaluation. First, an improvement in health status is equally good regardless of who receives it; second, the change in health status is universal (for example, mending a leg fracture produces the same level of benefit to all individuals regardless of whether they are an Olympic athlete or a frail elderly person). Finally, the change in health status can be observed by any individual who measures the change and is not open to different interpretations.

In economic evaluation, however, benefits of health care can be seen both as the improvement in well-being derived from an intervention, and more widely as the *value* that individuals place on better health for themselves and for others. Where an intervention produces a straightforward benefit which is widely seen as a good thing, such as mending a leg fracture, then the problem of *who* is to benefit and how society values that benefit is not seen as an important evaluation problem. Palliative day care, however, is an intervention that may provide different degrees of benefit for different kinds of people and is a contested area of health care. Under these circumstances, it may be helpful to move beyond a definition of benefit used in clinical evaluation. If it were possible to find out how patients and the public valued palliative day care, as opposed to other calls on society's resources, then this might produce a different kind of evidence for the benefits, or disbenefits, of palliative day care.

This means that it is necessary not only to measure changes in health status, but also to understand how individuals value a change in health status. This might be measured in how much they would be prepared to spend to improve their health or how much they feel the government should spend to move any person to a better health status. In seeing ways in which economics can assist in valuing palliative day care, two areas of economics are of particular relevance: welfare economics (Box 8.2) and consumer theory.

Box 8.2 What is welfare economics?

Economic evaluation is based on the economics of welfare. It is about the types and allocation of scarce resources in improving the health of the population. Health economists who work in the welfare economics tradition usually see the demand for health as a derived demand, that is, what individuals wants is good health in order to achieve other things, rather than an end in itself.

Vilfredo Pareto, a 19th Century Italian economist working mainly in Switzerland, set out the conditions under which change could lead to a social improvement in welfare in an economy. He stipulated that a change should be sanctioned where it made at least one person better off without making anyone worse off. A move towards these optimising conditions could be said to be an improvement in social welfare. His theory was further refined to say that if gainers in any change could compensate losers and there was still an improvement then there was an increase in social welfare.

Modern health economics is premised on these concepts of welfare. Health economic evaluation is the application of these criteria to health services. If a new intervention makes at least one person better off without making anyone else worse off (after they have been compensated) then the intervention should be adopted.

Consumer theory

In analysing demand for services it is normally asserted that individuals will voluntarily trade goods and services in order to make themselves better off. People are assumed to know which combinations of these will increase their welfare and act in a rational way to maximise their welfare for a given amount of resource. People as consumers are assumed to know, or have a very good idea of, the value of the goods and services they purchase and are best placed to make decisions about which combinations of goods and services will maximise their welfare. In principle, a consumer will buy and sell goods and services so as to get the most welfare from the resources available. If all consumers are well informed about the features of all goods and services, then they can buy and sell until no one would be better off by further voluntary trades. Exchange will continue until maximum welfare is attained.

An important point to emphasise here is that when an individual chooses a service, it is what the person wants given all the other choices available to them. It reflects how much a service is valued by an individual. In principle, then, if individuals and their advocates (in this case a doctor or a counsellor) were to be able to make decisions about how to use resources themselves, then they would maximise their welfare.

The notion that the individual is a well-informed consumer of health care has long been challenged, and this in part explains the presence of advocacy, regulation, subsidy and other interventions by government in the health sector. We can, however, draw on the understanding and preferences of patients to design better services. In particular, if the service focuses on improving quality of life for people with life-limiting illness and their families, then it is likely that the declared preferences of users will be of great value in planning service delivery.

Palliative day care encourages patients to use their autonomy to decide which type of therapies and activities they want to try. Patients and their advocates continually make decisions about which services are of benefit to them. The benefits of different interventions are not well understood, and not the same for all patients, therefore patients are encouraged to try a range of therapies. Their views about the benefits they derive from these services may be the best way of reflecting the true benefits derived from them.

Cost–benefit analysis (CBA)

The practical application of welfare economics in evaluation is cost–benefit analysis (CBA). CBA is a method of comparing costs and benefits in the same unit, usually money. This is a way of describing what people would be willing to sacrifice to have particular goods and services available. As a descriptor of reality, individuals' value of the consequences of an intervention can take into account any number of variables, known and unknown. These include attitudes to risk, attitudes to future health, and views on the benefits to other individuals. It compares health interventions with other uses of public and private resources. It implies that the benefits of an intervention do not have to be completely defined before the evaluation takes place. Influences on patients' welfare, which would not normally be taken into account, can be incorporated into the analysis. Therefore CBA allows all the important influences on demand for a service and future welfare from that service as perceived by the individual to be taken into account (Winch 1971).

This does *not* imply that individuals should be made to pay for services, that is, be charged what society has deemed the service to be worth, as this is a political decision. For example, in the UK patients are not charged for most NHS services, even though the cost of many services can be calculated and market testing could establish a price. To date, the British public has viewed payment as inequitable and prefers a tax-based system for financing most health care. It is a misconception that financial calculations for economic evaluation imply that patients should be charged for health care.

In addition, CBA does not imply that only the costs and benefits of a service that have a price tag should be counted. Monetary valuation provides a common currency for comparing the costs and benefits of health interventions with other calls on society's resources. CBA can provide information on whether an intervention represents better value, to individuals and to society, than other non-health care related interventions (such as summer holidays or education).

Applying economic evaluation to palliative day care

The economics of welfare and CBA are closely related to consumer theory (Mishan 1988). In health care, however, it is difficult to apply the methods of CBA because there are rarely market prices for the services offered (Drummond *et al.* 1997). Therefore it is not possible to observe how individuals make choices about their consumption based on relative prices of different goods and services. Other methods have to be developed which provide information on patients' valuation of health care based on asking them about how they would behave in hypothetical situations about health care use. A whole field of economic evaluation has developed to try and find appropriate methods of establishing the value of health services in this way (Donaldson 1990; Gafni 1997; Bala *et al.* 1998; Diener *et al.* 1998; Dolan 1999).

Are quality adjusted life years (QALYs) useful in palliative day care research?

In palliative day care the measurement of the benefits of an intervention is complex. Patients have multiple objectives, and are willing to trade-off different potential benefits. For example they may decide they would prefer better quality of life rather than simply prolonging their life with poor quality. They may make decisions to stop aggressive therapies that have distressing side-effects and to continue with palliation only. Evaluation methods that focus on only one of the possible dimensions of benefit (such as length of life) may miss other important factors.

Box 8.3 The quality adjusted life year (QALY)

A quality adjusted life year is a measure of health outcome or morbidity that can capture both the changes in morbidity (quality) and in mortality (years of life) from an intervention. It is a way of quantifying the outcome of a health care intervention by comparing the years of life saved and quality of life improved by the intervention with the same dimensions if the individual had not had the intervention.

The quality adjustment comes from multiplying years of life with a weight between 0 and 1. This weight represents a health state: 1 is perfect health and 0 is death. If a person is bed-ridden, this may be valued as a quality of life weight of 0.2. Ten years in this health states equals 10×0.2 QALYs, ie 2 QALYs. If a health intervention increases a persons life by another twenty years (i.e. stops premature mortality) and improves their quality of life to almost perfect health (say, 0.9, an increase of 0.7) then they will have gained 20×0.7, ie 14 QALYs.

The quality weights are derived from a number of techniques to reflect society's preferences for different types of health states. The types of people who are included in this exercise (patients, their carers, and the general public) can alter the final values placed on each health state.

Box 8.3 The quality adjusted life year (QALY) *(continued)*

The approach allows interventions which improve quality of life more than quantity of life (ie palliative care) to be compared with interventions which have a greater effect on morbidity (ie interventions that save lives of younger people).

There are critics of this approach, both in health economics and among health professionals. QALY analysis still favours interventions that prevent premature death: preventing a baby's death (saving about 70 years of life) will always produce more QALYs gained than a palliative care intervention, even one that dramatically improves a patients' quality of life. There is also criticism of any methodology that tries to reduce life to crude dimensions. In addition, there is scepticism about how these data will be used to rank interventions by how many QALYs they produce (and eventually to ration health care this way).

There is debate in health economics about the construction of quality of life weights (who decides what they should be and how health states are valued) and the theoretical basis for this approach. There is also concern about how data can be manipulated for political ends. Nevertheless, this approach when understood and used properly can provide some useful information about the relative benefits of health care interventions. It is an attempt to define benefit in a systematic way.

Economic evaluation tries to address this by developing research instruments that can incorporate more than one dimension of benefit. This has led to composite measures of benefit that combine longer life and improved quality of life. The best known instrument is the quality adjusted life year, or QALY (Loomes and McKenzie 1989; Mehrez and Gafni 1989). Box 8.3 describes how QALYs work and how they can be used.

The QALY is a measure of health gain from interventions rather than the *value* that individuals place on health gain. In classical economics the benefits of the consumption of goods and services can be measured by how much an individual would be willing to forego (in terms of giving up other goods and services, or money) in order to have the benefits of that intervention, as discussed in the previous section. That is, economists usually evaluate how much a person values the subjective benefits of consumption rather than measuring this is in an objective way. However, in health care, some economists have called for an abandonment of the quest to locate the measurement of benefits in terms of a value to individuals (Williams 1996). This argument focuses on health as an objectively quantifiable phenomenon, rather than as a derived, indirect means of obtaining subjective welfare. This is now labelled 'extra-welfarist economics' (Sen and Williams 1982; Culyer 1990).

For palliative care, differences in approaches to quantifying and valuing health gain matters. If a QALY is simply a measure of health status, then the standard approach (by asking individuals about changes in their health status over time) will not provide good evidence for decision-makers about palliative day care provision. Changes in health status are not expected to change dramatically in palliative day care (in comparison with acute care), and the QALY instrument is unlikely to be able to detect more subtle changes. The fact that patients may have a strong view about the value of benefits (or disbenefits) of palliative day care may not be adequately counted by a QALY measure (and other similar outcome instruments) which only captures predefined dimensions of health gain.

A return to CBA?

In principle, CBA allows comparisons to be made of the costs and consequences of diverse interventions in terms of how much individuals would be willing to pay for them. It is able therefore to capture all the dimensions of benefit of an intervention, both known and unknown. This is superior (if feasible study designs can be developed) to methodologies which only reflect predefined dimensions of benefit, such as the QALY. It would be of particular interest if the results of CBA studies differed markedly from the results of calculation of QALYs gained.

The current state of economic research evidence in palliative care

What is the quality of the evidence that already exists on the costs and benefits of palliative care?

Compared with other health sectors, there has been relatively little research on the economics of palliative care. One of the main problems relates to the difficulty of designing good quality research in palliative care, especially in the non-medical aspects of the service. This is not confined to economic evaluation; there is a dearth of good research evidence in palliative care more generally (see Chapter 9).

Measures of costs and benefits of palliative care can only be as good as the study design from which the data was extracted. As economic evaluation in palliative care is usually undertaken alongside clinical trials or observational studies, the quality of the evidence will depend to a large extent on the quality of the data from the main study.

As there has been almost no evaluative research undertaken on palliative day care, it is necessary to consider the economic evidence that exists on services in other types of palliative and terminal care delivery. A recent review of palliative care teams undertaken by the authors raised many of the questions that need to be addressed to improve the quality of economic evaluation of palliative day care (Higginson *et al.* 2000a).

The economic arm of the literature review found 14 studies in the international literature that contained data on costs and resource consequences alongside evidence of effectiveness. This was a sub-sample of the 43 studies identified in total. The economic criteria were taken from established guidelines for the publication of economic studies (Drummond *et al.* 1997). The majority of the studies (9 of 14) evaluated home care interventions; the others were of inpatient services, except one that was for a nurse co-ordination service. None of the studies evaluated palliative day care.

In the main, the evaluations included in the review were poorly executed and many of them failed to meet the basic standards for a good quality study. There were exceptions to this but on the whole, the published economic data do not produce strong evidence of cost-effectiveness. However, there are some important general points to make here about the quality of the evidence. The aims of the economic studies were to demonstrate lower costs of a palliative care service rather than relate this directly to clinical effectiveness or other benefits of different configurations of palliative care teams. Resource use was the only outcome measure considered in all but one study. This single study attempted to produce a utility-based measure (an unvalidated unit of benefit called a 'quality adjusted well-week'). This paper was methodologically weak and probably would not have been published if guidelines on economic evaluation had been available at the time of publication.

All the studies in the review avoided the problem of measuring benefit as the clinical study failed to demonstrate clear differences in effectiveness between any two interventions under comparison. It was therefore assumed that there were *no* other clinical or other type of benefit for patients from the intervention other than the defined outcome measured using a specific quality of life instrument. This was a big assumption. If a clinical effectiveness study fails to demonstrate a significant difference in one outcome, this is not the same as saying that there is no real difference in outcome, only that the research instrument employed has not found it. There is an important difference between these two states of knowledge and confusion between the two in evaluation studies can result in misleading conclusions.

As none of the studies in the review had seriously addressed the problem of measuring benefit, it could be argued that these studies started in the wrong place. By ignoring the benefit side of the cost-benefit equation they implicitly assumed that measuring the economic benefit of palliative care interventions was not a major part of the economic evaluation problem. This is not the case and is an important source of confusion in these studies.

The studies in the review demonstrate that the purpose of economic evaluation is poorly understood in a research community dominated by clinical research. The reason for this is that the outcome of interest in a clinical trial is fundamentally different from the outcome of interest in a full (CBA) economic study. In a clinical trial, the decision-maker has traditionally been interested in whether a patient (or a group of patients) has received better treatment than either a placebo or standard care. An economic evaluation (in the widest sense) considers whether the intervention is worthwhile (increases social welfare) and whether it should be adopted when compared with all other calls on the same resources, both in the health sector and in the economy as a whole. In order to assess this, wider measures of costs and benefits need to be considered than those included in clinical studies.

Current economic evaluation studies in palliative day care

The Thames regions palliative day care study incorporated an economic analysis of palliative day care (see Chapter 1). A pilot study was undertaken to assess the structure, process and outcomes of palliative day care in order to inform the methods of the main trial (Douglas *et al.* 2000). This was a necessary step in an area of health care where almost no economic work had been undertaken. This was the only published study that conducted a detailed analysis of the palliative care intervention to inform an economic evaluation.

The findings suggested that while there were some important differences in the way that palliative care was organised and the types of services that were offered to patients, many of the core services were similar across the centres. The study also found that different patients seemed to be using the services offered in palliative day care in different ways. Younger patients were seeking more active treatment, while older patients were less able or willing to try out new therapies. This implied that the characteristics of the patients, for example, their age, might have had a strong influence over the types of services they received and the subjective benefit they derived from it. Another observation that informed the economic evaluation was the way in which patients accessed services. While in NHS community and secondary care settings, patients may often have to wait for particular services, such as physiotherapy and counselling. In palliative day care centres, the emphasis was on providing patients with services when they required them, without keeping them waiting.

Differences in the organisation of care also translated into clinical services: doctors were usually available on-call to be consulted or available for clinical sessions. Similarly, specialist nurses were available every day in the units. As a result patients appeared to have better overall access to medical, nursing and therapeutic care than they might expect in other health care settings. At the same time, some services were under-utilised by patients who were too ill or tired to benefit from them even though they had appointments for specific therapies. This also contrasted with other health care settings, where patient appointments are often over booked to allow for patients who do not attend.

The flexibility and choice within the centres compared with other settings, and the way in which services were organised around the needs of individual patients meant that direct comparisons with NHS services could not easily be made.

These findings led to the consideration of other economic evaluation methods. These may provide different kinds of evidence of the effectiveness of palliative day care services which reflect the contrast of palliative day care with other types of specific, well defined, uni-dimensional interventions that are amenable to clinical trial evaluation.

New strategies for evaluating palliative day care

Problems with the standard approaches to economic evaluation in palliative day care has led to reconsideration of the important economic questions for evaluating a service. Rather than asking whether palliative day care is an effective intervention *in general*, it may be important to find out how to best meet patients' differing needs and how to assess the value they place on different kinds of services. For example, which combination of services should be provided to different groups of patients (older/younger, socially isolated/with carer support)? When should they be provided? Do different kinds of patients value different elements of palliative day care?

In seeking to answer questions such as these, techniques have been developed which ask individuals about their hypothetical willingness-to-pay for health care (Donaldson 1990; O'Brien and Viramontes 1994; Diener *et al*. 1998; Klose 1999). Respondents may be asked how much they think they would be willing to pay (or accept in compensation) for a particular health intervention or to move to a better or worse health state.

Using these techniques, respondents can be asked in one period of time how they value a service. There is no need for a comparison group, and the burden on patients and their families can be minimised. One approach in this family of techniques that may be particularly helpful in this context is called conjoint analysis, also known as discrete choice modelling (Ryan 1999). This is a promising technique that is being used in a number of different health care settings and may have important applications in palliative day care.

Conjoint analysis in palliative day care settings

Conjoint analysis is a tool for estimating patients' preferences for the individual characteristics of an intervention that has multiple characteristics or attributes, and that produces different kinds of outcomes as a result (Green and Srinivasan 1990).

Conjoint analysis specifies the characteristics of a health care service and attempts to establish which of these are valued over others (Ryan and Farrar 1995). By this means, it tries to get closer to assessing the value of complex characteristics of care from the users' point of view. A number of health care studies have been able to obtain reasonably good data from respondents using these methods. Use of conjoint analysis in palliative care has not yet been evaluated.

How conjoint analysis works

The important constituent parts of an intervention are determined from interviews with patients and carers, and conducting detailed observations of the service. Questionnaires can then be developed which reflect these characteristics. Patients are shown hypothetical descriptions of typical configurations of palliative day care services that are different in specific ways and then they are asked which one they would prefer to attend. Respondents are asked to make choices between a number of different palliative day care scenarios (perhaps 6 or 8 in an interview) and their responses indicate the relative importance of different aspects of palliative day care service to them. Information about the respondents which might also have an impact on their choice (such as their age, stage of illness and whether they live alone) are also gathered to assess whether they have any impact on their valuation of different aspects of palliative care.

The results of the study would show how much patients are willing to 'trade' (to use economic terms) between different aspects or characteristics of palliative day care and will indicate the relative value of different aspects of the service to users of the service. In palliative day care these characteristics may be as follows:

- appointment with a medical doctor available every attendance;
- availability of a hairdresser/possibility of having a bath every visit;
- other people of the same age at the centre;
- availability of group counselling;
- trained art co-ordinator available to run arts and crafts sessions;
- art therapists to run individual sessions;
- physiotherapy available every visit.

There are a number of reasons why conjoint analysis techniques might provide useful information in palliative day care research. First, experience during the Thames Regional Palliative Day Care study indicated that patients were willing and able to make choices about the service that contribute to their welfare. Second, staff reported that some patients valued some services to such an extent that they indicated they would be willing to pay for some of them if they were not provided free of charge. Third, although many patients were elderly, they did not suffer from cognitive impairment because this was frequently a criteria for refusing access to palliative day care. Consequently they were usually very willing and able to answer questions directly; they were also used to being asked their opinions.

Finally, this may be an innovative way of assessing patients' own valuation of particular aspects of the service in a way that has not been attempted before. There is ongoing debate in the field of palliative day care about the relative importance of various palliative day care activities and, during our fieldwork, strong views were expressed about the types of services that should be offered to patients. Conjoint analysis may be one way of eliciting patients' preferences for particular dimensions of care or activities that are difficult to obtain by other methods. The method is currently being piloted in a palliative day care study in the UK.

Conclusion

Different health care interventions have different costs and consequences. The aim of an economic evaluation of health care interventions and organisation is to set out the options available to purchasers and providers of health care in ways that are explicit and accessible. While economic evaluation cannot provide a 'right' answer, which will always depend in the end on the sway of political factors, and the values and beliefs of society, it can be a useful tool at many levels of policy analysis.

The normal question in any evaluation is 'should we or should we not implement this intervention?' Economic evaluation research in palliative day care has highlighted the need to redefine the questions we ask about health care interventions. There is little argument among the health care professionals that palliative day care provides a valuable service. However, what aspects of palliative day care makes it valued by patients is not well understood yet. Consideration of the problems of economic evaluation in this area can move the focus of attention away from 'does it work?' to 'what is most valued by the patients themselves—under what conditions, and for whom?'

New economic methods are developing which may be very useful and are already being tested in palliative day care settings. These methods take into account respondents' valuation of the expected benefits to them from palliative day care. It provides a way of undertaking evaluation where the individual's preferences are still at the centre of the evaluation process.

In the field of palliative care, economic evaluation is still relatively new and underdeveloped. This may make some people wary of the value of undertaking economic evaluation. However, as long as the technical problems can be understood and the conclusions of any study reflect the constraints of undertaking research in this area, economic research can help palliative care to compete on a par with other services for scarce health service resources.

Summary points

♦ Economic evaluation of palliative day care is becoming more inevitable as centres compete for resources with other forms of palliative care and other health services.

♦ Economic theory provides a good basis for evaluating palliative day care services in different ways from other forms of evaluation, and for answering different kinds of questions.

♦ There has been almost no economic evaluation of palliative day care in the UK and the economic studies of other forms of palliative care are mostly undertaken poorly and with little understanding of the purpose of economic evaluation of health care.

- Traditional economic evaluation methods may not perform well in studies where the intervention is complex, has multiple objectives and dimensions, and where the outcomes are not easily defined.

- Techniques of economic evaluation that are relatively new to health care may provide useful information to decision-makers about the value of different combinations of palliative day care services to defined groups of patients.

- Research is now underway which is developing these methods of economic evaluation in palliative day care settings.

References

Abel, E. K. (1986). The hospice movement: institutionalising innovation. *International Journal of Health Services*, **16**, 71–85.

Bala, M. V., Wood, L. L, Zarkin, G. A., Norton, E. C., Gafni, A. and O'Brien, B. (1998). Valuing outcomes in health care: a comparison of willingness-to-pay and quality-adjusted life-years. *Journal of Clinical Epidemiology*, **51**, 667–76.

Bayer, R., Callahan, D., Fletcher, J., Hodgson, T., Jennings, B., Monsees, D., Sieverts, S. and Veatch, R. (1983). The care of the terminally ill: morality and economics. *New England Journal of Medicine*, **309**, 1494.

Billings, J. (1998). What is palliative care? *Journal of Palliative Medicine*, **1**, 73–81.

Culyer, A. J. (1990). Commodities, characteristics of commodities, characteristics of people, utilities and the quality of life. In *Quality of life: perspectives and policies*. (ed. S. Baldwin, C. Godfrey and C. Propper), pp. 9–27. Routledge, London .

Department of Health (1996). *A policy framework for commissioning cancer services: a report by the expert advisory group to the Chief Medical Officers of England and Wales*. HMSO, London.

Department of Health (2000). *The National Cancer Plan*. Department of Health, London.

Diener, A., O'Brien, B. and Gafni, A. (1998). Health care contingent valuation studies: a review and classification of the literature. *Health Economics*, **7**, 313–26.

Dolan, P. (1999). Valuing health-related quality of life: Issues and controversies. *Pharmacoeconomics*, **15**, 199–27.

Donaldson, C. (1990). Willingness to pay for publicly-provided goods. A possible measure of benefit? *J Health Economics*, **1**, 103–118.

Douglas, H.-R. Higginson, I. J., Myers, K. and Normand, C. (2000). Assessing the structure, process and outcome in palliative day care: a pilot study for a multicentre trial. *Health and Social Care in the Community*, **8**, 336–44.

Drummond, M. F., O'Brien, B., Stoddart, G. L. and Torrance, G. W. (ed.) (1997). *Methods for the economic evaluation of health care programmes.* Oxford University Press, Oxford.

Gafni, A. (1997). Willingness to pay in the context of an economic evaluation of healthcare programs: theory and practice. *American Journal of Managed Care,* **Suppl.**, S21–32.

Goddard, M. K (1989). The role of economics in the evaluation of hospice care. *Health Policy,* **13,** 19–32.

Goddard, M. K. (1993). The importance of assessing the effectiveness of care: the case of hospices. *Journal of Social Policy,* **22,** 1–17.

Grande, G. E., Todd, C. J., Barclay, S. I. G. and Doyle, J. H. (1996). What terminally ill patients value in the support provided by GPs, district and Macmillan nurses. *International Journal of Palliative Nursing,* **2,** 138–43.

Green, P. and Srinivasan, V. (1990). Conjoint analysis in marketing: new developments with implications for research and marketing. *Journal of Marketing,* **4,** 3–19

Higginson, I. J., Finlay, I. G., Goodwin, D. M., Cook, A. M., Edwards, A. G. K., Hood, K., Douglas, H-R. and Normand, C. E. (2000a). *The role of palliative care teams: a systematic review of their effectiveness and cost-effectiveness.* (Unpublished report to the Welsh Office), Department of Palliative Care and Policy, King's College London; Velindre NHS Trust; Department of General Practice UWCM.

Higginson, I. J., Hearn, J., Myers. K. and Naysmith, A. (2000b). Palliative day care: what do services do? *Palliative Medicine,* **14,** 277–86

Jarvis, H., Burge, F. I., Scott, C. A. (1996). Evaluating a palliative care program: methodology and limitations. *Journal of Palliative Care,* **12,** 23–33.

Klose, T. (1999). The contingent valuation method in health care. *Health Policy,* **47,** 97–123.

Loomes, G. and McKenzie, L. (1989). The use of QALYs in health care decision-making. *Social Science and Medicine,* **28,** 299–308.

Mehrez, A. and Gafni, A. (1989). Quality-adjusted life years, utility theory and health-years equivalents. *Medical Decision-making,* **11,** 140–6.

Mishan, E. J. (ed.) (1988). *Cost-benefit analysis.* Unwin Hyman Ltd., London.

Normand, C. E (1996). Economics and evaluation of palliative care. *Palliative Medicine,* **10,** 3–4.

O'Brien, B. and Viramontes, J. L. (1994). Willingness to pay: a valid and reliable measure of health state preference? *Medical Decision Making,* **14,** 289–97.

Payne, S. A. (1996). Perceptions of a good death. *Palliative Medicine,* **10,** 307–12.

Robbins, M. A. (1998). The economics of palliative care. In *Oxford textbook of palliative medicine,* (ed. D. Doyle, G. Hanks and N. MacDonald), pp. 55–65. Oxford University Press, Oxford.

Ryan, M. (1999). Using conjoint analysis to take account of patient preferences and go beyond health outcomes: an application to *in vitro* fertilisation. *Social Science and Medicine*, **48**, 535–46.

Ryan, M. and Farrar, S. (1995). A pilot study using conjoint analysis to establish the views of users in the provision of orthodontic services in Grampian. Health Economists' Study Group Meeting, University of Bristol, Bristol.

Salisbury, C., Bosanquet, N., Wilkinson, E. K., Franks, P.J., Kite, S., Lorentzon, M. and Naysmith, A. (1999). The impact of different models of specialist palliative care on patients' quality of life: a systematic review. *Palliative Medicine*, **13**, 3–17.

Sen, A. and Williams, A. (ed.) (1982). *Utilitarianism and beyond*. Cambridge University Press, New York.

Spencer, D. J. and Daniels, L. E. (1998). Day care hospice—a review of the literature. *Palliative Medicine*, **12**, 219–29.

Tierney, A. J. and Sladden, S. (1994). Measuring the costs and quality of palliative care: a discussion paper. *Palliative Medicine*, **8**, 273–81.

Torrens, P. R. (1984). Studies in hospice economics. *Medical Care*, **22**, 289.

Whynes, D. (1997). Costs of palliative care. In *New themes in palliative care*, (ed. D. Clark, J. Hockley and S. Ahmedzai), pp. 34–59, Oxford University Press, Oxford.

Williams, A. (1996). QALYs and ethics: a health economist's perspective. *Social Science and Medicine*, **43**, 1795–804.

Winch, D. (ed.) (1971). *Analytical welfare economics*. Penguin, London.

PART D. CHALLENGES FOR DAYCARE

9

Future perspectives for day care

Kathryn Myers

The infrastructure of buildings and services needed to provide specialist palliative care to most of the UK has been developing for 30 years and is now well established. In some places a range of services is available, providing more options and choices to both purchasers and recipients of palliative care than at any other time. The environment in which these services operate, however, is changing.

First, the population itself is ageing. This will bring an increase in diagnoses of cancer, which is predominantly a disease of the elderly, and an increase in the numbers of those living with other chronic medical conditions (Quinn and Babb 2000). Although people are living longer than ever, there has been no apparent reduction in ill health or disability in the elderly (Dunnell and Dix 2000), so palliative care services are likely to find themselves involved in the care of larger numbers of elderly people. Along with these demographic changes, it is probable that more palliative care will be provided by non-specialists in the future and that the trend to care for people in the community—in their own homes or in nursing homes—will continue.

Second, expectations of health services and people's attitudes towards them are changing. Funders are increasingly concerned about quality, effectiveness and value for money when purchasing health care. Processes of care are coming under greater scrutiny, with increasing emphasis on providing for the needs and choices of patients through the provision of individualised packages of care (Bosanquet and Salisbury 1999, p. 9). In addition, specialist palliative care services are being challenged to broaden the range of patients for whom they provide and to integrate more fully with mainstream primary and secondary care services.

Palliative care services, including day care, cannot afford to remain static if they are to survive and prosper in this changing environment. This chapter aims to explore some of the major forces for change and outline possible ways in which day care services in particular might respond.

Forces for change

The challenge to demonstrate effectiveness

The 'evidence-based' movement has well and truly arrived. There is increasing pressure on all types of health care services to provide evidence for their effectiveness and cost-effectiveness. Demand for services is increasing, patients expect to be treated as effectively as possible, and the requirements of purchasers need to be satisfied. Therefore it is important to know what the best treatments are and how to deliver these in the most efficient ways to the greatest number likely to benefit. In this climate the establishment of a comprehensive evidence base to demonstrate the effectiveness and cost-effectiveness of palliative day care is becoming increasingly urgent. Building such an evidence base is not easy and has hardly begun. A recent 270 page review aimed at identifying the most appropriate and cost-effective models of service delivery and level of provision of palliative care services included just two short paragraphs relating to day care and failed to identify any studies related to the evaluation of palliative day care services (Bosanquet and Salisbury 1999).

The dearth of evidence that relates to the effectiveness of palliative day care might have several causes. One is that palliative day care may have been seen as self-evidently such a 'good thing' and so clearly beneficial to those attending that time-consuming and costly research has been considered unnecessary. Another reason for the lack of evidence could be that palliative day care is a complex service and good research into its effectiveness will also necessarily be complex, requiring time, expertise and funding. As will be discussed further below, the types of evidence that it is possible to obtain about palliative care services often differ from the types used to measure effectiveness in other medical disciplines. It has been only recently, with the emergence of academic departments of palliative care, that the possibility of conducting complex research into palliative care services has become a reality. The need for Government funding of research into palliative care has been recognised (Science and Technology Committee 2000), and, should this materialise, the opportunities it will afford will be widely welcomed.

The challenge to prove quality

In 1997 the Government White Paper 'The new NHS. Modern. Dependable' (Department of Health 1997) spelled out the need for all health services to ensure that they deliver care of the highest quality. The following year, the consultation paper 'A first class service. Quality in the new NHS' (Department of Health 1998) expanded further upon how quality improvement through clinical governance would work in practice. While there is no legal obligation for voluntary sector hospices to introduce clinical governance, most receive some NHS funding and will therefore be expected to put in place arrangements to assure the quality of care offered (Tebbit 2000). The quality of palliative day care services, like their effectiveness, can no longer be inferred as self-evident but must now be demonstrable and open to scrutiny.

The role of audit as a corner stone in clinical governance and the monitoring of quality has already been described by Hearn in Chapter 7. Before quality can be measured, however, it must be defined. Quality of care is a complex and multidimensional concept and a great deal has been written about its definition and characteristics. One helpful and well recognised model is that developed by Maxwell (1984). He identified six core components: effectiveness, acceptability, efficiency, access, equity and relevance to need, later combining them with the concepts of structure, process and outcome proposed by Donabedian (Donabedian 1980, Maxwell 1992). This form of analysis has subsequently been applied in a number of health care settings, including palliative care (Armes and Higginson 1999) in which it can be important to examine both the processes and outcomes of care in order to reflect the quality of service being delivered.

Box 9.1 contains a brief outline of Maxwell's model with some additional example questions that might be applicable to a palliative day care service. Many of the concepts outlined by Maxwell are useful as starting points for audit and as a checklist when planning new service developments. Several components of the model highlight however, that demonstration of quality is heavily reliant on the need for evidence about what constitutes best practice, and for validated outcome measures that reliably reflect the impact of services on patients and their carers. Whilst the definition of best practice remains elusive (Tebbit 2000) and validated outcome measures that assess patients' global experience of palliative care services are few and far between, measurement of quality in palliative care services will remain a challenge.

Box 9.1 Defining quality in palliative day care

Effectiveness: is the service the best available in the technical sense? Are the professionals involved competent, skilled, and knowledgeable? Do they have access to adequate support and ongoing training? What is the overall result for patients of receiving the service?

Acceptability: how humanely and considerately is the service delivered? What do patients think of it? Can they be sure of privacy and confidentiality? Is the service culturally sensitive? Is it equally acceptable to both men and women? Why is the service unacceptable to those who come once or twice but then no more?

Efficiency: is the output maximised for a given input? For example, is the centre operating at most efficient occupancy of places? Is there significant duplication of services with other providers? Is there effective co-ordination of care and communication with other service providers?

Access: can patients access the service when they need it? What are the barriers to access, for example, restricted opening hours, difficulties with providing transport or a waiting list? Is the service flexible and responsive to individuals' needs?

Equity: is one type of patient being treated more or less fairly than another? Is there discrimination, however unwitting, because of a patient's underlying diagnosis, language or cultural preferences? Are interpreters and special diets always available to those that want or need them?

Relevance to need: is the overall pattern and balance of services the best that could be achieved, taking into account the needs and preferences of the population as a whole? To what extent is the service needs led and person-centred rather than service led?

Adapted from Maxwell (1992) and Armes and Higginson (1999).

The challenge of generic palliative care

Calls to extend appropriate palliative care services to patients with diagnoses other than cancer (so-called generic palliative care) have been made for some time (for example SMAC/SNMAC 1992), but with relatively little impact on specialist palliative care services to date. In the United Kingdom in 1995, less than 4% of all patients cared for by palliative home or day care services or newly referred for inpatient care (excluding services that specialise in children or HIV/AIDS) had a diagnosis other than cancer (Eve *et al.* 1997).

The various issues surrounding the provision of palliative care services for people with non-malignant diseases have been well described (George and Sykes 1997, Wasson 2000) and are summarised in Box 9.2. Whilst there has been understandable reluctance to extend the scope of palliative care services when existing resources already appear to be at full stretch, the issue of the inequity of the present situation will not go away. It is undoubtedly true that some patients with cancer are able to access a range of specialist palliative care services whilst the majority with other diagnoses 'the disadvantaged dying' (George and Sykes 1997), receive no specialist services at all. A great deal of work remains to be done to determine the needs of patients dying from non-malignant disease and their carers, but it cannot be disputed that, when considered individually, some of these patients, regardless of age, have considerable symptoms and physical needs (Addington-Hall and Karlsson 1999). It is also highly likely that some patients with non-cancer diagnoses have needs for information related to their diagnosis. Some may have the same kinds of anxieties and spiritual and social issues related to death and dying as patients with cancer. Some might well benefit just as much from the social, creative and therapeutic opportunities offered in palliative day care as patients with cancer.

Anxieties have been expressed that even small numbers of patients with incurable non-malignant diseases might overwhelm palliative care services because of their uncertain and relatively long prognoses, and that the current high standards of care for cancer patients would therefore be compromised (Gannon 1995, Beattie *et al.* 1995). Such anxieties and the issues from which they arise need to be addressed in ways other than excluding patients from services altogether. Estimating the prognosis in many patients with cancer is known to be difficult and is frequently inaccurate (Christakis and Lamont 2000). Improvements in treatments are turning some cancers into chronic diseases. Already a significant proportion of patients with cancer attend palliative day care services for long periods. In the Thames regions survey 29% of the patients attending palliative day care centres in one particular week had been attending for over a year and the mean attendance of the longest-stay patients at the palliative day care centres questioned was 4.5 years (range 1–12 years) (Higginson *et al.* 2000). The reasons why some patients with cancer remain in palliative day care for such long periods of time have not been studied.

Box 9.2 Generic palliative care

Reasons for extending palliative care services to patients with diagnoses other than cancer:

- it is unethical to discriminate against patients on the grounds of diagnosis alone;

- all patients should be treated on the basis of their needs not their diagnosis;

- some patients with diagnoses other than cancer are likely to have physical, emotional, social, informational and spiritual needs that require specialist palliative care services;

- the carers of these patients may need support, information and respite services.

Reasons for reluctance to extend services:

- existing resources are limited and both statutory and voluntary funding may be less forthcoming for patients with diagnoses other than cancer;

- the needs and preferences of patients with diagnoses other than cancer and their carers are presently poorly defined and largely unquantified;

- the role of existing specialist palliative care services in meeting the needs of these patients is presently poorly defined;

- patients' prognoses may be less clear cut and the terminal phase harder to define, leading to uncertainty about the appropriate timing of provision of specialist palliative care;

- fears that services may be swamped and standards compromised;

- lack of confidence, knowledge and specialist resources amongst professionals;

- reluctance to change practice into areas where professionals perceive lack of expertise.

Adapted from George and Sykes 1997, and Wasson 2000

There may be inadequate processes for ongoing needs assessment, review and discharge in some palliative day care centres. In addition, some patients may have needs related more to poor social circumstances, loneliness, isolation or bereavement, all fairly common among the elderly population in general, rather than specific to having cancer. Nevertheless, discharging such patients is extremely difficult because alternative less specialist services that they might move on to often do not exist.

In this context, it appears particularly unfair that some who have, or have had cancer are able to benefit from relatively long term specialist palliative care support whilst others with different diagnoses receive no support at all. The challenge for palliative day care services on this issue is twofold. First, to develop processes to identify the needs and preferences of all patients who have life-threatening illness, regardless of the underlying diagnosis and to keep these under review as patients' situations change. Second, to create a diverse range of services that integrates more extensively with other parts of the health and social care network, so that patients changing needs can be fully met at all times. This will be discussed further below.

Whatever objections might be raised to the concept of generic palliative care, the future of some palliative care services may hinge on this issue. In the National Cancer Plan, the Government pledged an extra £50 million for investment in hospices and specialist palliative care services by 2004 (Department of Health 2000) but this was contingent on broadening access to core services to more patients, including those with non-cancer diagnoses.

The challenge of funding

There have been significant changes to the ways in which palliative care services are funded in recent years. First, primary care trusts have been devised as major commissioners of health care. Second, the level of support that palliative care services have enjoyed from the voluntary sector appears to have been changing and certainly cannot be guaranteed to the same degree in the future. Both these factors will have significant implications for the future of palliative day care.

Purchasing of services by primary care trusts

In 1997 the government announced major changes to the commissioning of local health services through the creation of primary care groups (Department of Health 1997) and, since 1 April 2000, primary care trusts (PCTs) (NHS Executive 1999). Through this legislation, family doctors and other members of the primary care team have been given greater powers over the development and commissioning of both community and secondary health services.

The effects of these changes on palliative care services are yet to be fully realised. Indeed, there may be very positive benefits. Greater emphasis on community services may direct more resources into palliative care. The emergence of long-term service agreements to replace annual contracts could allow much greater security and certainty in strategic planning of service developments. These changes may also represent a threat to some palliative care services. While local situations and priorities may show considerable variation, it is not inconceivable that the determination of priorities by PCTs may undermine the existing balance and integrated nature of some palliative care services. Some PCTs may, for example choose to fund more home care at the expense of services such as day care. A questionnaire study of 167 GP principals and 96 registered district nurses carried out in the Cambridge area demonstrated that these two professional groups had very different priorities when asked about the importance and adequacy of local palliative care services. Both doctors and district nurses ranked palliative day care in the bottom three out of a list of eleven local palliative care services in terms of priority (Barclay et al. 1999). Another questionnaire survey of 31 GPs demonstrated a desire for increased home nursing services, particularly at night, greater access to services for patients with diagnoses other than cancer and improved access and availability of hospice beds (Hanratty 2000). No mention was made of palliative day care. The extent to which findings such as these will be reflected in the purchasing priorities of PCTs cannot be predicted.

Changes in funding from the voluntary sector

The profile of charitable giving in the UK appears to be changing and some well-established medical charities have suffered as a result. The emergence of the National Lottery may have had a part in this process, as might the ageing of the population as more people make provision to support themselves in older age. The effect on palliative care funding from the voluntary sector is not yet known. Help the Hospices is presently carrying out a questionnaire survey of independent hospices in the United Kingdom that in part seeks to investigate any changes in the amount and sources of voluntary funding of hospices (D Praill, personal communication). Whilst many independent providers of palliative care may be able to maintain current levels of voluntary funding, they may not be able to raise the extra resources needed to meet increasing demands upon them.

How can palliative day care services respond
The challenge of research

A recurring theme in the above sections is that far more needs to be known about the effectiveness of palliative day care—how it is effective, for whom and under what circumstances—if it is to meet the challenges it faces. This information can only be provided by high quality, rigorous research. It has been recognised for some time however that palliative care is not easily amenable to research using the methodologies held up as 'gold standards' in other medical disciplines (Aradna 2000). Major challenges lie not only in developing alternative methodologies, but also in educating those requiring evidence for the effectiveness of palliative day care that the types of evidence it is possible to offer will differ from the types offered in support of many other health care interventions.

The difficulties that beset research into palliative care in general have been well documented and are summarised in Box 9.3.

In addition, palliative day care presents unique challenges to the researcher:

- the 'therapeutic environment' of day care cannot easily be described or defined, neither is it easily amenable to dissection into individual components;
- the experience of palliative day care involves relationships with staff and other patients unique to this type of care and is more complex than the sum of individual therapeutic interventions;
- measuring intangible 'outcomes' such as the effects of palliative day care on patients' self esteem, confidence and hope, and describing and evaluating the human relationships that contribute to the value of day care is not straightforward;
- different palliative day care centres practise different models of care and offer different ranges of services;
- different patients within one centre may receive very different 'packages' of care both because care is tailored to individuals needs and because different services may be available on different days;
- there is no consensus about the definitions of particular activities, for example 'art therapy' in one centre may mean participation in a creative project supervised by nurses or untrained volunteers or one-to-one therapy with a professional art therapist in another;
- palliative day care is rarely the only health service being used by patients and different health services may make different contributions to patients' well being at different times.

Box 9.3 Methodological difficulties in conducting palliative care research

♦ Potential participants may be physically and emotionally vulnerable.

♦ Exclusion and inclusion criteria might introduce bias into samples and results might not be generalisable.

♦ The uncertain nature of the disease process can result in poor accrual, high attrition and difficulties in timing outcome measurements.

♦ Matching of subjects in comparative studies can be difficult.

♦ Defining and maintaining contrasts between different models and strategies for the duration of a study can be difficult.

♦ Data collection and interpretation may be affected by the role of the researcher.

♦ Many traditional health care indices are inappropriate for use in palliative care.

♦ Measurement tools vary in reliability and validity.

♦ There is a wide choice of outcome measures but the lack of a 'gold standard'.

♦ There are ethical difficulties related to randomisation of palliative treatments.

♦ Use of carers as proxies in providing assessments is unreliable.

Adapted from Rinck 1997, Gotay 1983, McWhinney 1994 and Salisbury and Bosanquet 2000.

In spite of these potential difficulties, the need to evaluate remains. In 1996 Corner outlined a new model for palliative care research, describing it as responsive, collaborative, inclusive and multi-method. Others have underscored the need for creative approaches and the combination of research techniques, calling for well conducted observational studies, careful descriptions of the context and processes of care and the use of qualitative methods alongside well-validated quantitative techniques. Large-scale trials in palliative care are also likely to be more conclusive and a better investment in the long term than smaller ones (Salisbury and Bosanquet 2000). Such large-scale studies require considerable collaboration between professionals of different disciplines. Staff in palliative day care may find themselves working alongside researchers, academics, health economists, sociologists and statisticians amongst others. The use of independent researchers is particularly important because members of staff in palliative day care can themselves be a crucial component of the therapeutic process.

Key issues for research

Potential areas for research in palliative day care are legion. Some key questions include:

♦ **What actually happens in palliative day care?** The Thames regions palliative day care study has provided a beginning here through a detailed description of five UK services and the processes of care that happen within them (Higginson *et al.* 2000; Douglas *et al.* 2000).

♦ **What are the benefits of palliative day care? Which groups of patients and carers benefit most and under what circumstances?** Answering these questions will require detailed descriptions of the costs and benefits of palliative day care to different groups of patients and carers, including those with diagnoses other than cancer. Is palliative day care, for example, particularly beneficial to those who live alone or to those with very newly diagnosed or very advanced disease? Identifying those that benefit most will enable services to be targeted more efficiently in future. The choice of outcome measures will, however, be crucial. Some measures of outcome commonly used in assessments of patients' quality of life, particularly those focusing on physical symptoms and functioning, may not fully reflect the experience of patients attending palliative day care services. New measures of outcome that take into account benefits described by patients, such as improved self esteem and reduced social isolation, need to be developed and used alongside qualitative techniques if the full impact of palliative day care is to be assessed.

♦ **Are there particular components of palliative day care services that bring about greater benefits than others?** Whilst different palliative day care centres offer different models of services, all offer core services of social interaction and respite from usual daily life (Douglas 2000). What are the relative contributions of these core services, and any additional ones, to the benefits gained by patients attending palliative day care?

♦ **To what extent does palliative day care meet the needs and preferences of particular groups of patients? Are there groups of patients that are excluded from current palliative day care services, and why?** As described by Gunaratnam in Chapter 3, some patients may feel excluded or uncomfortable in palliative day care because their particular cultural needs and philosophies of life are not fully recognised. Others may be excluded simply because the right type of transport cannot be provided. Research into the reasons why some patients attend palliative day care only once or twice before 'dropping out' might be very revealing of a range of patient needs and preferences that existing palliative day care services are failing to meet.

+ **To what extent does palliative day care substitute, supplement or duplicate other health and social services that patients might receive?** Little is known about how palliative day care services fit into and interact with this wider web of resources and services. The Thames regions palliative day care study may provide some preliminary answers to this question.

+ **To what extent do the philosophies and perceptions of health professionals determine the types of patients that attend and the types of needs that individual centres seek to meet?** In the absence of an evidence base and rigorous local needs assessments, some palliative day care services may have developed according to the philosophies and perceptions of service providers rather than in response to patients' needs. The existence of this 'philosophy–needs' gap has been highlighted by Spencer and Daniels (1998) and has already been referred to by Gunaratnam in Chapter 3. The key issues are whether and how health professionals differ from patients in their perceptions of needs, requirements for services and outcomes. In other words, do patients and carers receive what they really need from services, or what the service providers think they need? Do services actually achieve for patients what their providers think they achieve? These are not easy questions to ask, let alone answer. They involve challenging views and assumptions, sometimes dearly held. It is widely held for example, that respite care provides a break for carers. This is undoubtedly true in many cases. There has been no research, however, into whether this is always true (for some, getting a patient ready for a day at the day centre in time may be a cause of increased stress), or how useful the break is in terms of its timing or duration.

The information to be gained through research is essential to the development and funding of future palliative care services. Whilst the scrutiny of services by teams of researchers may appear threatening to those who provide them, rigorous research may in fact lead to significant support for many palliative treatments and to the development of new services which may benefit a larger number of patients (Normand 1996).

The challenge of diversification

There is little doubt that palliative day care services will need to make imaginative responses to the needs of broader groups of patients in the future. This may mean greater flexibility in the ways that existing services are provided and possible diversification of the models of care offered. Examples of this might include:

- extension of the availability of services by opening centres in the evening and at weekends for day care, or making the premises available 'out of hours' for related activities such as counselling or patient support groups;
- provision of new services, e.g. the introduction of a bathing service by a centre that previously offered only creative and social activities;
- co-ordination with inpatient services to allow overnight stays;
- the designation of particular days for patients with particular needs, for example young patients, those who have diagnoses other than cancer, or those with behavioural difficulties—while this might enable special needs to be met most effectively, the danger that particular groups may feel stigmatised or discriminated against by such a policy needs to be borne in mind;
- provision of 'drop-in' day care sessions where patients, particularly those recently diagnosed, can access support and information;
- greater use of information technology to provide information for patients about their illness and available services—this might be particularly important for patients with diagnoses other than cancer for whom information is sometimes less readily available;
- variable patterns of day care intervention, e.g. 'holiday at home' services, whereby patients attend daily for two weeks every three or four months;
- development of 'peripatetic' services—these would visit community locations such as the mosque or temple in order to access groups of patients who might feel uncomfortable visiting the 'hospice', and might have no specific day care building to operate from. Likewise mobile day care services based in a different location every day might serve patients in a widely spread geographic area or in nursing homes.

The challenge of patient review and discharge

Increasing pressure on services might lead to re-examination of the open-ended policy for day care attendance that has frequently operated in some palliative day care centres in the past. Some palliative day care centres make a contract with patients and their referrers at the outset of day care attendance that they will attend for a specific period of time and with specific goals in mind. Before the end of the contract, a review is conducted to decide whether further attendance or referral on to other agencies would be most beneficial.

Many practitioners in the field recognise that discharging patients from a much appreciated palliative day care service can be difficult for all concerned. One hospice established a patient support group for those discharged from day care (Johnson 2001). Others have found themselves taking initiatives in partnership with other agencies such as social services in order to ensure that their own specialist services are used most appropriately yet patients' needs are still met.

The challenge of integration

Most palliative day care services are integrated to a greater or lesser extent with other local specialist palliative care services, such as an inpatient unit or community palliative care team. It is not uncommon for patients' care to move between components of this integrated service as their needs change. Palliative day care services are also part of a wider network of primary and secondary health services and social services that are available to patients. As more patients with a wider range of diagnoses require palliative care, this network is likely to increase in size and complexity. Palliative day care services will need to integrate as fully as possible with this network if it is to function to the best advantage of the largest number of patients. This is particularly true when patients needs border on the ill-defined interface between health and social care.

The challenge of meeting the needs of patients with diagnoses other than cancer will require the forging of partnerships and new alliances between health care professionals in a variety of fields if patients are to receive specialist palliative care when they require it. Though by no means widely available, rehabilitation and home care services for patients with chronic, neurological, cardiac or respiratory diseases have already been developed in some areas, independent of local specialist palliative care services. Enormous scope exists for partnership in such initiatives. Specialist palliative care professionals might be a valuable source of education, expertise, inspiration and support, whilst learning and gaining experience and confidence with new groups of patients themselves. This might lead to more patients with diagnoses other than cancer using existing specialist palliative care services, or to the development of new services for these patients within primary and secondary health care and community settings.

In an ideal world, patients with life-threatening illnesses would be able to move freely between specialist palliative care, primary and secondary health services with each service fully aware of the roles of the others, and each fully aware of changes in the patients' condition and treatment. Developing such partnerships in practice, however, will require a far greater level of communication and information exchange than exists in most health service networks at present. More extensive and imaginative use of information technology to communicate rapidly and confidentially between health professionals will be critical. The prize will be an integrated network of health and social services able to deliver individualised packages of care that are responsive to individual patients' changing needs. Palliative day care services may find themselves at the centre of such a network, if they are able to remain flexible and truly led by the needs of each patient.

Summary points

- The population is ageing and more older people will be living with cancer and other life-threatening diseases in the future.
- Palliative day care services will come under increasing pressure to demonstrate the effectiveness and quality of the services they provide.
- The needs of patients with diagnoses other than cancer will need to be taken into account to a much greater extent in the future, and services adapted or developed accordingly.
- Research is essential if palliative day care services are to meet the needs of the greatest numbers of people in the most effective ways.
- Diversification and integration with other health and social services will be crucial if palliative day care services are to be extended to broader groups of patients in the future.

References

Addington-Hall, J. M. and Karlsen S. (1999). Age is not the crucial factor in determining how the palliative care needs of people who die from cancer differ from those of people who die from other causes. *Journal of Palliative Care*, 15, 13–19.

Aradna, S. (2000). Changing paradigms in research: do we need to rethink the future? *Progress in Palliative Care*, 8, 193–7.

Armes, P. J. and Higginson, I. J. (1999). What constitutes high-quality HIV/AIDS palliative care? *Journal of Palliative Care*, 15, 5–12.

Barclay, S., Todd, C., McCabe, J. and Hunt, T. (1999). Primary care group commissioning of services: the differing priorities of general practitioners and district nurses for palliative care services. *British Journal of General Practice*, **49**, 181–6.

Beattie, J. M., Murray, R. G., Brittle, J. and Catanheira, T. (1995). Small numbers of patients with terminal cardiac failure may make considerable demands on services. *British Medical Journal*, **310**, 1411.

Bosanquet, N. and Salisbury, C. (1999). *Providing a palliative care service. Towards an evidence base.* Oxford University Press, Oxford.

Christakis N and Lamont E. (2000). Extent and determinants of error in doctors' prognoses in terminally ill patients: prospective cohort study. *British Medical Journal*, **320**, 469–72.

Corner J. (1996). Is there a research paradigm for palliative care? *Palliative Medicine*, **10**, 201–8.

Department of Health. (1997). *The new NHS: Modern. Dependable.* Department of Health, London.

Department of Health. (1998). *A first class service. Quality in the new NHS.* Health Services Circular 1998/113. Stationery Office, London.

Department of Health. (2000). *The National Cancer Plan.* 2000/0532. Department of Health, London.

Donabedian, A. (1980). *The definition of quality and approaches to its assessment.* Ann Arbor, Michigan: Health Administration Press.

Douglas, H.-R., Higginson, I. J., Myers, K. and Normand, C. (2000). Assessing structure, process and outcome in palliative day care: a pilot study for a multicentre trial. *Health and Social Care in the Community*, **8**, 336–44.

Dunnell, K. and Dix, D. (2000). Are we looking forward to a longer and healthier retirement? *Health Statistics Quarterly*, **6**, 18–25.

Eve, A., Smith, A. M. and Tebbit, P. (1997). Hospice and palliative care in the UK 1994–5, including a summary of trends 1990–5. *Palliative Medicine*, **11**, 31–43.

Gannon, C. (1995). Palliative care in terminal cardiac failure. Hospices cannot fulfil such a vast and diverse role. *British Medical Journal*, **310**, 1410–1.

George, R. and Sykes, J. (1997) Beyond cancer? In *New Themes in Palliative Care*, (ed. D. Clark, J. M. Hockley and S. Ahmedzai), pp. 239—53. Open University Press, Buckingham.

Gotay, C. C. (1983). Models of terminal care: a review of the research literature. *Clinical Investigations in Medicine*, **6**, 131–41.

Hanratty, B. (2000). GP views on developments in palliative care services. *Palliative Medicine*, **14**, 223–4.

Higginson, I. J., Hearn, J., Myers, K. and Naysmith, A. (2000). Palliative day care: what do services do? *Palliative Medicine*, **14**, 277–86.

Johnson, L. (2001). Time to move on. *Hospice Bulletin*, **8**, 4.

Maxwell, R. J. (1984). Quality assessments in health. *British Medical Journal*, **288**, 1470–1.

Maxwell, R. J. (1992). Dimensions of quality revisited: from thought to action. *Quality in Health Care*, **1**, 171–7.

McWhinney, I. R., Bass, M. J. and Donner, A. (1994). Evaluation of a palliative care service: problems and pitfalls. *British Medical Journal*, **309**, 1340–2.

NHS Executive. Primary Care Trusts. (1999). *Establishing Better Services*. HMSO, London.

Normand, C. (1996). Economics and evaluation of palliative care. *Palliative Medicine*, **10**, 3–4.

Quinn, M. and Babb, P. (2000). Cancer trends in England and Wales. *Health Statistics Quarterly*, **8**, 5–19.

Rinck, G. C., van den Bos, G. A. M., Kleijnen, J., de Haes, H. J., Schade, E. and Veenhof, C. H. N. (1997). Methodological issues in effectiveness research on palliative cancer care: a systematic review. *Journal of Clinical Oncology*, **15**, 11697–707.

Salisbury, C. and Bosanquet, N. (2000). Assessing palliative care is difficult. *British Medical Journal*, **320**, 942.

Science and Technology Committee (2000). *Cancer research—a fresh look*. Sixth report of the science and technology committee, 25 July 2000. Para 117. The Stationery Office, London.

SMAC/SNMAC (Standing Medical Advisory Committee and Standing Nursing Advisory Committee). (1992). *The principles and provision of palliative care*. HMSO, London.

Spencer, D. J. and Daniels, L. E. (1998). Day Hospice care—a review of the literature. *Palliative Medicine*, **12**, 219–29.

Tebbit, P. (2000). *Raising the standard. Clinical governance for voluntary hospices*. Occasional paper 18. National Council for Hospice and Specialist Palliative Care Services, London.

Wasson, K. (2000). Ethical arguments for providing palliative care to non-cancer patients. *International Journal of Palliative Nursing*, **6**, 66–70.

INDEX

acceptability 139
accessibility 35, 139
actualisation 60
administrative support 57
advocates 23
African-Caribbeans 26
Africans 26
ageing population 136, 143
age of patients 6, 19, 128–9, 148
AIDS 19
anxiety 64
aromatherapy 63
arts 67–74
art therapy 50, 65
art workshops 69, 71
Asian patients 24, 25, 26, 27
Attenborough Report 67
audit 53, 94–115
  antipathy towards 104
  costs and benefits 98–9, 106
  cycle 95–6
  data analysis 109
  defined 94–5
  establishing 107–8
  examples 96–7
  hope 76
  implementing results 106, 109
  management of 104–5
  objectives 106
  reports 109
  research and 97–8
  staff cooperation 104
  success 108
  tools 100–4
  training 105–7

Australia 5, 54
awareness raising 12

Bangladeshi patients 25–6, 37
behavioural difficulties 8, 148
best practice 138
black patients 24, 25, 26, 27, 31
brochures 55

cancer 6, 9, 16, 19, 26, 81, 88, 136
  ethnicity and 26
  journey 88
  National Cancer Plan 142
  prognosis 140
  rehabilitation 89
  symptom prevalence 16, 17
capital replacement 56
care package 80, 85
carers 46, 48
case studies 71, 73
categorical thinking 33, 38
chaplaincy 66, 87
charities 116–17; see also voluntary
  sector
Chinese 31
client-centred therapy 59
clinical governance 138
collaboration 82
communication 51, 82

community-based palliative care 25–6
community health services 9
community support services 66
comparative need 12
complementary therapies 63, 82, 96
confidence 64
conjoint analysis 130–1
consumer theory 122
cost-benefit analysis 122–3, 126
cost-effectiveness 5
counselling 66
crafts 73
creative arts 67–74
creative writing 73–4
cultural factors 12; *see also* ethnicity

data
    analysis 109
    collection 53–5
    presentation 109
death, *see* mortality
demands 12, 13
depression 64
'disadvantaged dying' 28, 140
discharge policy 9, 56, 76–7, 149
discrete choice modelling 130
discussion groups 65–6
disease
    outcomes 99–100
    patterns 20
diversification 148
diversional therapist 50
doctors 6, 49, 79–93
    role 80–3
    skills 83–5
documentation 84
drop-in services 6, 148

economic benefit 120–1
economic evaluation 123–4, 126–9
economics 116–35

Edenhall Marie Curie Centre 85–9, 90
Edmonton Symptom Assessment Schedule 102
education 23, 50–1, 83, 97
effectiveness 10, 19–20, 137, 139
efficiency 139
epidemiological-based needs assessment 13, 14–17
equity 28–32, 139
ethnicity 23–42
    categorization 31–2
    equity and need 28–32
    mortality patterns 28
    recording of 30–1
    service use 25–6
    under-utilisation 26–7
European Organisation for Research on Treatment of Cancer Quality of Life Questionnaire 102
evaluation 9–10, 53, 75–6, 116, 118–24, 126–9
evidence-based approach 137
exclusion criteria 8, 46
extra-welfarist economics 126

'First class service. Quality in the new NHS' 138
food preferences 33–4, 37
'Framework for Cancer Care' 89
fulfilment 66–75
funding 6, 19, 56–7, 117, 137, 142–3

gardening 74
'gate-keeper' 8, 83
generic palliative care 139–42
group discussion 65–6

hairdressing 50, 52, 64
hair loss 63, 64

health economics 116–35
health service use 13, 14
health status 120, 121
Hebrew Rehabilitation Centre for Aged
    Quality of Life Index 102
Help the Hospices 143
hierarchy of needs 60
history taking 83–4
HIV 19
'holiday at home' 148
holistic care 28–9
home care 7
hope 76
horticulture 74
hospice/hospice care 1, 2, 8, 14, 90
Hospice Information Service 19
hospice palliative day care 2
human capabilities 36
humour 35, 75

incidence 15
information technology 148, 150
Initial Assessment of Suffering 102
inpatient care 7, 8, 51, 88–9, 148
integration 7, 149–50
interpreters 23, 26

language problems 26
laughter 75
lived experiences 32–4
longevity 136

McGill Quality of Life Questionnaire
    102
McMaster Quality of Life Scale 102
management plans 84
marketing 8, 55–6
Maslow 60, 77
massage 63

media 55
medical history 83–4
medical intervention 79–80
medication 51
mental illness 64
minimum data set 53–5
mobile day care services 148
mortality
    patterns 28
    rates 15
motor neurone disease 19
multidisciplinary teams 3, 80–1, 82,
    86–7
music 74
music therapy 50, 65
Muslims 34, 37

National Cancer Plan 142
National Hospice Study 19–20
needs
    defined 12–13
    equity and 28–32
    hierarchy 60
needs assessment 5, 12–22, 43, 45
    aims 12
    epidemiological methods 13,
        14–17
    health service use 13, 14
'New NHS. Modern. Dependable' 38
non-malignant disease 16, 17, 19, 28,
    81, 88, 139–42, 149
normative need 12
notes 53
nurses 6, 49, 62, 64

occupational therapists 50
office space 52
official launches 55
open days 56
'Opening Doors' 24, 25
opening hours 6, 148
operational policy 47–8

outcome measures 96, 98, 99–104, 144, 145
outdoor access 52
'out of hours' activities 148

package of care 80, 85
palliative care 2
Palliative Care Assessment tool 103
Palliative Care Core Standards 103
'Palliative Care for All' 27–8
Palliative Care Outcome Scale 100, 103
palliative care services 2
palliative day care
 centre size 6
 characteristics 6–7
 complexity 3
 criticisms of 1
 definitions 1, 2
 diversification 148
 diversity of 118
 effectiveness 10, 19–20, 137, 139
 establishing 43–58
 evaluating 9–10, 53, 75–6, 116, 118–24, 126–9
 exclusion criteria 8, 46
 expansion 4–5, 14
 flexibility 3
 impact on other services 8–9
 integrated 7, 149–50
 international provision 5–6
 misconceptions 7
 objectives 18–19
 relationship to other services 7–8
 surveys 6–7, 18–19
 UK provision 4–5
patients
 age 6, 19, 128–9, 148
 assessment 83–4
 interactions 7
 numbers cared for 6, 19
 review 56, 148–9
 satisfaction 100
pattern recognition 84
peripatetic services 148
personal appearance 63–4

pharmacy services 51
philosophy-needs gap 147
physiological needs 62
physiotherapists 50, 86
policies 47–8
pottery 68–9
premises 52
prescriptions 51
prevalence 16, 17
primary care trusts 142–3
problem avoidance 56–7
psychiatric nurses 64
psychosocial day care 59–78
psychosocial factors 30, 31
publicity 8
purchasers 95, 142–3

qualitative research 110, 145
quality adjusted life years (QALYs) 124–6
quality of care 138–9
quality of death 118
quality of life 86, 100, 101

race equality 23
referral
 criteria 8, 45–6
 forms 48
 indications for 87–8
 patterns 83
 reasons for 17
 routes 7, 48
reflexology 63
rehabilitation 89
religion 66
reminiscence 74–5
research 110, 126–9, 137, 144–7
 and audit 97–8
resources 56–7, 98–9, 118
risk management 83
Rodgers 59, 77
Rotterdam Symptom Checklist 103

safe practice 82–3
St Christopher's Hospice 23
    Day Care Centre 59–78
St Christopher's Nurses at Home
    62
St Luke's Hospice 3
Schedule for the Evaluation of
    Individual Quality of Life 103
'seamless service' 5, 7
self-care 63
self-esteem 63, 64, 66–75
service network mapping 45
service specification 46–7
social death 60
social exclusion 34–8
social factors 12
social inequalities 36–8
social isolation 35
social workers 50, 66
specialist palliative care services 2
specialist palliative day care 2
spiritual care 59
staffing
    administrative support 57
    composition 49–51
    ethnic diversity 23
    levels 48
    responsibilities 49–51
    see also doctors; nurses
stigma 66
supply and demand 13
support 66, 80–1, 149
    discussion groups 65–6
Support Team Assessment Schedule 103
surveys 6–7, 18–19
symptom
    control 81
    prevalence 16, 17
Symptom Distress Scale 103

talking 35-6
taxis 52
team working 3, 80–1, 82, 86–7
television 55
Thames regions palliative day care
    study 6, 7, 9, 118, 120, 128, 146
therapeutic model of care 85–9, 90
therapies, new 20
training 23, 105–7
transport 8, 35, 52

United Kingdom
    death rates 15
    palliative day care provision 4-5
United States of America 5, 35

'value added' services 50
voluntary sector 5, 116, 117, 143
volunteers 48, 50, 52, 68
    education 50–1
    handbook 51

weight change 63
welfare economics 121
willingness-to-pay 130

young patients 6, 128, 148